Pattern Cross-Examination

Questions for Sexual Assault Cases:

A Trial Strategy & Resource Guide

Michael Waddington & Alexandra González-Waddington
Attorneys at Law

Pattern Cross-Examination Questions for Sexual Assault Cases: A Trial Strategy & Resource Guide

Michael Waddington & Alexandra González-Waddington

1792 Bell Tower Ln #218

Weston, FL 33326

www.ucmjdefense.com

Pattern Cross-Examination Questions for Sexual Assault Cases/ Michael Waddington & Alexandra González-Waddington -- 1st ed.

ISBN-9798344995540

Disclaimer:

By using this book, you acknowledge that you have read this disclaimer and agree to its terms.

Purpose and Limitation of Content:

The content provided in this textbook is for educational and informational purposes only and is not intended to serve as legal advice. It should not be used as a substitute for consultation with a professional legal advisor. While we strive to provide timely and accurate information, we make no representations or warranties regarding the applicability, accuracy, completeness, or suitability of the information contained within this book for any particular legal situations. The information may not reflect the most current legal developments.

Professional Legal Consultation:

Readers are advised to seek professional legal counsel regarding any specific legal issues or questions they may have. This book should not be used as the sole basis for making legal decisions. No action or inaction should be taken based solely on the contents of this information. Always consult with a qualified attorney regarding your legal matters.

No Attorney-Client Relationship:

Accessing this book, as well as using any of its content or resources, does not create an attorney-client relationship between the reader and the book's authors or publishers. Such a relationship can only be established through a direct and explicit agreement.

Disclaimer of Liability:

The authors, publishers, and contributors to this textbook expressly disclaim all liability with respect to actions taken or not taken based on any or all of the contents of this book. The book is provided "as is," without warranty of any kind, either express or implied, including but not limited to the accuracy, reliability, or completeness of the information.

Use of Content:

The responsibility for the application of any information taken from this textbook rests solely with the reader. The authors and publishers are not liable for any misuse of the material or any adverse consequences from the application of the information provided herein. It is the reader's responsibility to ensure that their use of this information complies with current laws and regulations in their jurisdiction.

Intellectual Property Rights:

All content within this book is the property of the authors and publishers unless otherwise noted. Unauthorized use of the material without express consent is prohibited.

ALSO BY THE AUTHORS

- *Pattern Cross-Examination Questions for Expert Witnesses: A Trial Strategy & Resource Guide*

- *Pattern Cross-Examination for DNA and Biological Evidence: A Trial Strategy & Resource Guide*

- *Battlemind: A Military Legal Thriller*

- *Kick-Ass Closings: A Guide to Giving the Best Closing Argument of Your Life*

- *The Art of Trial Warfare Volume II: Applying Sun Tzu's The Art of War to Modern Litigation*

- *The Art of Trial Warfare: Winning at Trial Using Sun Tzu's The Art of War*

- *Trial Warrior's Book of Wisdom: A Compilation of Quotes for Success in Law and Life*

TABLE OF CONTENTS

TABLE OF CONTENTS IN DETAIL

INTRODUCTION

Throughout our careers as lawyers, we have defended hundreds of people accused of sex crimes and various other criminal offenses. The majority of these cases were tried before a jury. In our experience, adverse witnesses, law enforcement, experts, and forensic examiners often embellish their testimony at trial. Many prosecution witnesses see themselves as advocates, as members of the prosecution team. Some witnesses will do whatever is necessary to win and send the defendant to prison. This may include lying, exaggerating, and misstating facts. When a witness is willing to lie or embellish their testimony in order to win, innocent people often, unfortunately, end up in prison.

This book is designed to give defense lawyers pattern cross examination questions that can be easily modified and used in a variety of sexual assault cases. Our goal is to shorten the learning curve, and help defense lawyers effectively cross examine challenging witnesses without having to reinvent the wheel with each new case. The questions in this book serve as a starting point. Because every case is different, the cross examiner should modify the questions based on the facts of their case.

This book is not a textbook on the theories of cross examination. Our samples are based on various cross examination techniques, primarily those found in *Cross-examination: Science and Techniques,* by Larry Pozner and Roger J. Dodd. In order for these techniques to be effective, and to maintain witness control, you must ask good questions. Ask only leading questions, with one new fact per question, and break cross examinations into logical progressions towards specific goals. The cross examiner should gain and maintain witness control, and not back down until the witness answers the question.

A note regarding the use of the word "victim." In this book, the word "victim" is used to make the questions easier to follow. In trial, replace the word victim with "complaining witness," "alleged victim," "accuser," or the person's name (i.e. Ms. Jones).

In addition, throughout the book you will notice that we generally refer to the "victim" as "she." While both males and females can be victims of sexual crimes, we have used "she" for consistency and ease of reading. In trial, choose the word "he" or "she" as appropriate.

Cross-examining victims can be daunting, even for seasoned attorneys. Victims often have strong emotions and may hold deep-seated perspectives on the events in question. Effectively cross-examining a victim requires a command of the subject at issue and the ability to maintain control throughout the testimony. If the victim senses that the cross-examining lawyer is nervous, unprepared, or inexperienced, they may take control of the cross-examination. Some may attempt to dominate the exchange, refuse to answer direct questions, or deliver lengthy explanations to sway the jury. A patient, unemotional, disciplined, and well-prepared lawyer can bring even the most challenging witnesses back on track. When appropriately cross-examined, victims who exhibit bias may lose credibility.

For the techniques tin this book to be effective, and to maintain witness control, you must adhere to these rules:

1. Prepare and have your impeachment resources available (prior statements, depositions, learned treatises, etc.);
2. Remain calm and unemotional;
3. Do not answer questions posed to you by the expert (they are the ones testifying, not you);
4. Ask only leading questions;
5. Insert only one new fact per question;
6. Break cross-examinations into logical progressions towards specific goals;
7. Gain and maintain witness control; and
8. Do not back down until the witness answers the question you asked.

REFERENCES

For more information on cross-examination techniques, we recommend the following:

- *Cross-examination: Science and Techniques*, by Larry Pozner and Roger J. Dodd.

- *Look-Good Cross-Examination Audio Course*, by Terence MacCarthy.

- *MacCarthy on Cross-Examination*, by Terence MacCarthy.

- *Masters of Cross-Examination DVD,* by Larry Pozner and Roger J. Dodd.

- *The Art of Trial Warfare: Winning at Trial Using Sun Tzu's The Art of War*, by Michael S. Waddington.

CHAPTER 1: DEALING WITH DIFFICULT WITNESSES

Never argue with stupid people, they will drag you down to their level and then beat you with experience.
-Mark Twain

In sexual assault cases, the majority of the prosecution's witnesses are adverse and hostile. They are biased against the accused. They are hostile towards the defense. When cross-examining adverse or hostile witnesses, it is common for the witness to avoid answering the question asked. They will often give non-responsive answers or quibble over basic facts.

The cross examiner must be persistent, and not allow the witness to avoid answering the question. Here are techniques to use when cross-examining difficult witnesses. The defense lawyer should strive to remain calm and professional when using these techniques. Do *not* be baited by the witness and stoop to their level, or engage in petty bickering.

Technique 1: Repeat the question.

This technique is used when the witness is non-responsive and refuses to answer simple questions. When the witness gives a non-responsive answer, repeat the question, slowly and clearly. Repeat this several times until the witness gives a responsive answer. After two or three times, it does not matter what answer the witness gives, they lose credibility with each evasive answer.

Example 1:

Q: You said that Steve violently raped you?
A: Yes, he did.

Q: After Steve violently raped you, you returned to his house?

A: Listen, I was under a lot of stress. You know victims react differently, and sometimes they do things that may seem odd.

Q: After Steve violently raped you, you returned to his house?

A: I know what you're trying to do, make me look bad. But you don't know what it is like until you've been through something like this.

Q: After Steve violently raped you, you returned to his house?

A: Blah, blah.

Q: After Steve violently raped you, you returned to his house?

A: Yes.

Example 2:

Q: You returned to his house the next evening?

A: What was I supposed to do? I left my phone there.

Q: You returned to his house the next evening?

A: I needed my phone for work.

Q: You returned to his house the next evening?

A: Blah, blah.

Q: You returned to his house the next evening?

A: Yes.

Example 3:

Q: You returned to his house alone?

A: Well, I didn't want to wake up my roommate.

Q: You returned to his house alone?

A: I didn't know anyone else that I could call.

Q: You returned to his house alone?

A: Blah, blah.

Q: You returned to his house alone?

A: Yes.

Technique 2: Repeat twice and then reverse.

This technique is used when the witness is non-responsive and refuses to answer simple questions. The key is to allow the witness to give the non-responsive answer and then repeat the question, slowly and clearly. Repeat the question twice, and then ask the question in the negative.

Example 1:

Q: You returned to his house?

A: What was I supposed to do? I left my phone there.

Q: You returned to his house?

A: I needed my phone for work.

Q: You never returned to his house?

A: I did, because I needed my phone.

Q: You did return to his house?

A: Yes.

Example 2:

Q: You returned to his house alone?

A: Well, I didn't want to wake up my roommate.

Q: You returned to his house alone?

A: I didn't know anyone else that I could call.

Q: When you returned to his house, you brought someone with you?

A: No, I didn't.

Q: You returned to his house alone?

A: Yes.

Technique 3: So your answer to my question is "Yes."

This technique is used when the witness is non-responsive and refuses to answer a simple question. When a witness gives a non-responsive answer, you will ask, "So your answer to my question, 'INSERT QUESTION,' is yes?" This puts the witness on the spot and they often concede the answer.

Example 1:

Q: You returned to his house?

A: What was I supposed to do? I left my phone there.

Q: So your answer to my question, "you returned to his house," is yes?

A: Yes.

Example 2:

Q: You returned to his house alone?

A: Well, I didn't want to wake up my roommate.

Q: So your answer to my question, "you returned to his house alone," is yes?

A: Yes.

Technique 4: Perhaps I did not make myself clear.

This technique is used when the witness is non-responsive and refuses to answer a simple question. When a witness gives a non-responsive answer, let them finish with their answer. When they stop talking, state, "Perhaps I did not make myself clear. The question I asked you was, 'INSERT QUESTION?' What is your answer to that question?" When using this technique, some witnesses will continue to ramble. If so, then use one of the techniques mentioned above. Either way, the witness is losing credibility in front of the jury by being non-responsive.

Example:

Q: You returned to his house?

A: What was I supposed to do? I left my phone there.

Q: Perhaps I did not make myself clear. The question I asked was, "you returned to his house?" What is your answer to that question?

A: Blah, blah.

Technique 5: Did you hear the question I just asked you?

This technique is used when the witness is non-responsive and refuses to answer a simple question. When a witness gives a non-responsive answer, let them finish with their answer. When they stop talking, ask, "Did you hear the question I just asked you?" Regardless of their answer, repeat the question.

Example:

Q: You returned to his house?

A: What was I supposed to do? I left my phone there.

Q: Did you hear the question I just asked you?

A: Yes or No.

Q: You returned to his house?

A: Blah, blah.

Technique 6: There are lot's of things you want to tell the jury.

This technique is used when the witness is non-responsive and refuses to answer a simple question. When a witness gives a non-responsive answer, let them finish with their answer. After they stop talking, state, "I understand there are a lot of things you want to tell the jury. But my question was, 'INSERT QUESTION.' What is your answer to that question?"

Example:

Q: You returned to his house?

A: What was I supposed to do? I left my phone there.

Q: I understand there are a lot of things you want to tell the jury. But my question was, "You returned to his house?" What is your answer to that question?

A: Blah, blah.

Technique 7: Does something prevent you from answering yes or no?

This technique is used when the witness is non-responsive and refuses to answer a simple question. When a witness gives a non-responsive answer, ask, "Is there something about my question that prevents you from answering yes or no?"

Example:

Q: You returned to his house?

A: What was I supposed to do? I left my phone there.

Q: Is there something about my question that prevents you from answering yes or no?

A: Yes or no.

Q: You returned to his house?

A: Blah, blah.

Technique 8: Are you finished yet?

This technique should only be used on obnoxious, but harmless witnesses. Do not use this technique on harmful witnesses who want to blurt out prejudicial information. Use it when the witness is non-responsive and the jury is growing tired of their rambling responses.

Example:

- -

Q: When they left the bar, they were holding hands?

A: There were a lot of people coming and going out of the bar that night. I mean, it was a Friday night. We were so busy we were just trying to keep our heads above water. Blah, blah.

Q: When they left the bar, they were holding hands?

A: Blah, blah, non-responsive.

Q: When they left the bar, they were holding hands?

A: Blah, blah, non-responsive.

Q: Anything else you want to add?

A: Blah, blah, non-responsive.

Q: Are you finished?

A: No.

A: Blah, blah, non-responsive.

Q: When they left the bar, they were holding hands?

A: Blah, blah.

Q: When questioned by the police, you told them that when they left the bar, they were holding hands?

These techniques will aid in dealing with difficult and adverse witnesses. Practice them repeatedly so you can incorporate them into your cross examinations at will.

CHAPTER 2: CROSS EXAMINING THE ALLEGED VICTIM

Cross examining an alleged victim in a sexual assault case can be a daunting task. When doing so, you must be professional and polite, and keep your questions simple.

COACHED TESTIMONY

In most sexual assault cases, the prosecution will rehearse both the direct, and the cross-examination with the alleged victim. They will coach the witness on how to answer and how to avoid answering certain questions. If you suspect a witness has been coached, you should consider cross-examining on this topic to highlight the coaching to the jury.

Point: The witness was coached by the prosecution.

Q: Before today, you discussed your testimony with the prosecutor?

A: I mean, I talked to her, yes.

Q: Before today, you talked to the prosecutor about what you would say on the witness stand?

A: We talked about what happened.

Q: You talked about what you would say on the witness stand?

A: About what happened?

Q: You talked about what you would say on the witness stand?

A: Yeah.

Q: Before today, you met with the prosecutor 5 times?

Note: From this point forward, assume the witness is non-responsive and evasive. Use the techniques taught in Chapter 1 to deal with adverse witnesses and make them answer the question asked. For the sake of brevity, below are the main points that should be made during the cross examination.

Q: You have spent at least 5 hours meeting with the prosecutor?

Q: The prosecutors gave you tips on what to say on the witness stand?

Q: The prosecutors gave you tips on how to say it?

Q: The prosecutors gave you tips on how to look believable?

Q: The prosecutors gave you tips on how to answer?

Q: The prosecutors gave you tips on how to dress for court?

Q: You came to this courtroom before today?

Q: You sat in the chair that you're sitting in now?

Q: While you were sitting in that chair, the prosecutor asked you questions?

Q: The prosecutor went over the questions that you would be asked in court?

Q: The prosecutor went over your answers?

Q: They gave you tips on how to answer better?

Q: They gave you tips on how to sound more believable?

Q: They prepared you for your testimony?

Q: You discussed questions that I might ask?

Q: You went over potential cross-examination questions?

Q: The prosecutor gave you tips on how to answer my questions?

Q: The prosecutor gave you tips on how to sound believable?

A: They told me to tell the truth.

Q: You spent 5 hours with them preparing and they only told you to tell the truth?

Q: Do you usually have to practice telling the truth?

Q: Whose idea was it to practice telling the truth?

Q: Do you usually practice before you tell your wife/husband the truth?

Q: Do you usually practice before you tell your boss the truth?

Q: Do you remember any time, in your life, when you needed to practice telling the truth, except in this case?

SEXUAL ASSAULT WHERE THE VICTIM IS INTOXICATED

Could the victim make cognitive decisions?

When defending a case involving a victim that claims to have been too drunk to consent, it is not necessary to show that the witness was sober. In most jurisdictions, an intoxicated person can consent, if they are able to make cognitive decisions. Often, prosecutors take on cases where the witness was drinking and engaged in consensual sexual behavior only to regret it later. The standard is not whether the victim made a good decision, but whether he or she was mentally and physically capable of making a decision.

A person that is unconscious, asleep, or rendered incapable of consent due to the ingestion of alcohol or drugs cannot consent.

Where the victim is able to make cognitive decisions and consents to engage in sexual behavior, the lawyer must highlight the victim's ability to think, act, communicate, and control his or her body. Furthermore, in a case involving alcohol facilitated sexual assault, the drinking habits and history of the victim are crucial. This is particularly true where the victim claims that her memory was impacted by the alcohol.

Point: The victim has a tolerance to alcohol.

Q: You drink alcohol?

Q: You drink alcohol frequently?

Q: You started drinking alcohol when you were 17 years old?

Q: You are currently 22 years old?

Q: You have been drinking alcohol for the past five years?

Q: On average, you drink 5-7 drinks per evening?

Q: You drink 2-3 days a week?

Q: You drink on weekends?

Q: You drink when you go out to clubs with your friends?

Q: You drink alcohol at home?

Q: You have a high tolerance for alcohol?

Point: Victim makes bad decisions while drinking.

Q: When you drink, you sometimes do things you would not normally do?

Q: When you drink, you sometimes do things that are out of character?

Q: When you drink, you sometimes act differently?

Q: When you drink, you sometimes make bad decisions?

Q: When you drink, you sometimes do things you later regret?

Q: When you drink, you sometimes say things you later regret?

Point: Victim's personality changes when drinking.

Q: You are normally a quiet person?

Q: You are shy?

Q: You sometimes feel shy in social settings?

Q: When you drink alcohol, you sometimes act differently?

Q: You become less shy?

Q: You become more social?

Q: You become more outgoing?

Q: The more you drink, the more social you become?

Q: When you drink, you sometimes do things you would not normally do?

Point: Victim cannot remembering actions while drinking generally.

Q: When you drink, you sometimes have trouble remembering what you did?

Q: When you drink, you sometimes have trouble remembering what you said?

Q: When you drink, you sometimes have trouble remembering how you acted?

Q: When you drink, you sometimes have trouble remembering details of the evening?

Q: Sometimes you remember parts of what you said and did?

Q: Other parts you cannot remember?

Q: The more you drink, the less you remember?

Point: Victim cannot remembering actions on the night in question.

Q: On the night of the alleged rape, there are certain parts of the evening that you cannot remember?

Q: You cannot remember everyone you talked to?

Q: You cannot remember everything that you said?

Q: You cannot remember everything that you did?

Q: For example, witnesses saw you dancing on the table, but you say that you do not remember dancing on the table?

Q: You may have been dancing on the table?

Q: You just have no memory of it?

Q: You are aware that witnesses saw you dancing with (name of the accused)?

Q: Witnesses saw you grinding with (name of the accused)?

Q: Witnesses saw you kissing (name of the accused)?

Q: You claim that you do not remember dancing with (name of the accused)?

Q: You claim that you do not remember grinding with (name of the accused)?

Q: You claim that you do not remember kissing (name of the accused)?

Q: As far as you know, you may have danced with (name of the accused)?

Q: You may have grinded with (name of the accused)?

Q: You may have kissed (name of the accused)?

Q: You don't deny that that happened?

Q: You just claim to have no memory of it?

Point: Victim acts differently when drinking but still chooses to drink.

Q: You know that when you drink, you act differently?

Q: When you drink, you do things that you don't normally do?

Q: When you drink, sometimes you act wild?

Q: When you drink, you sometimes do things you regret the next day?

Q: Especially if you drink 5-7 drinks?

Q: Knowing how you act when you drink, you still go out drinking at least once a week?

Q: Sometimes more?

Q: Knowing how you act when you drink, you still drink 5-7 drinks when you go out?

Q: Nobody forces the alcohol down your throat?

Q: Nobody forces you to go out and drink every weekend?

Q: You make those choices?

Point: Victim was in control of her body.

Q: On the night of the alleged sexual assault, you wore high heels to the club?

Q: The heels were about four inches long?

Q: You were able to walk in the high heels?

Q: You were able to dance in the high heels?

Q: You danced in the high heels after drinking 5 alcoholic drinks?

Q: You danced to several songs after drinking 5 alcoholic drinks?

Q: You did not fall down while dancing?

Q: No one had to hold you up while you were dancing?

Q: You had control of your body at the club?

Q: You had control of your body while you danced?

Q: You were in full control of your body while at the club?

Q: You left the club at 2AM?

Q: When you decided to leave the club, you were still wearing the high heels?

Q: You walked out of the club wearing the high heels?

Q: At the front of the club, there is a set of stairs?

Q: There are about 25 steps in that flight of stairs?

Q: The stairs lead down to the street?

Q: The stairs are not well lit?

Q: They are made of concrete?

Q: You walked down that flight of stairs?

Q: In your high heels?

Q: You did not trip walking down the stairs?

Q: You did not fall walking down the stairs?

Q: You did not stumble walking down the stairs?

Q: You walked down the stairs on your own?

Q: You were in control of your body when you walked down the stairs?

Q: When you reached the street level, you walked to your friend's car?

Q: The car was parked two blocks away?

Q: You walked two blocks to the car without help from your friend?

Q: You did not fall?

Q: You did not stumble?

Q: You were in control of your body when you walked to the car?

Q: When you arrived at the car, the door was locked?

Q: You waited for your friend to open it?

Q: Then you pulled the door open?

Q: You got into the car and sat down?

Q: Then she drove back to campus?

Q: It was a 20-minute car ride?

Q: When you arrived at campus, your friend parked the car?

Q: You got out of the car?

Q: You walked to your dorm?

Q: Your dorm is a five-minute walk from the parking garage?

Q: When you got to the dorm, the security guard asked to see your ID?

Q: You heard him?

Q: You understood him?

Q: You were not confused about what he said?

Q: You were not confused about what he had asked for?

Q: When he asked for your ID you opened your purse?

Q: You looked through your purse for the ID?

Q: You looked until you found it?

Q: You then gave the ID to the guard?

Q: The guard scanned the ID?

Q: While the guard scanned the ID, you waited until he gave the card back?

Q: After he gave your ID card back you entered the dorm?

Q: Your room was on the second floor of the building?

Q: You then walked up a flight of stairs to your room?

Q: You were still wearing high heels?

Q: The same high heels as you wore when you danced at the club?

Q: When you walked up the flight of stairs to your dorm, you did not stumble?

Q: You did not fall?

Q: You did not trip?

Q: You did not need help walking?

Q: You were in control of your body, physically, the entire time?

Q: You had no trouble finding your room?

Q: You were able to remember your room number?

Q: Your mind was able to comprehend what you were doing at the time?

Q: You clearly understood that you were looking for your room?

Q: Your room was locked?

Q: You needed a key to enter the room?

Q: You realized that when you arrived at the room?

Q: You looked for the keys in your purse?

Q: You found your keys?

Q: You had seven keys on the keychain?

Q: You remembered which key was the key to your room?

Q: You inserted the key into the lock?

Q: You opened the door and entered the room?

Q: When you entered the room, you realized that you were in your room?

Q: At that time, if it was not your room, would you have known?

Q: Your brain was able to understand where you were?

Q: You understood what you were doing?

ALLEGED MEMORY LOSS

In many sexual assault cases, especially when alcohol is involved, the victim will claim to remember all, some, or none of the events in question. In reality, their may or may not remember everything that happened. However, when a victim remembers some of the details but claims to forget facts that show that she consented to the sexual acts or that the defendant may have had a mistake of fact as to consent, then the cross examiner must highlight the memory loss because it impacts the victim's credibility demonstrates her ability to perceive and accurately remember what happened.

Point: Victim remembers certain details but not others.

Q: You remember going to the club?

Q: You remember what drinks you ordered?

Q: You remember how many drinks you ordered?

Q: You remember drinking a Miller Lite?

Q: You remember having a cherry Jell-O shot?

Q: You remember drinking another Miller Lite?

Q: You remember talking to your friend Jean?

Q: You remember that the accused was in the club?

Q: You remember seeing him?

Q: You remember him staring at you?

Q: You remember him creeping you out?

Q: You remember thinking that he was not attractive?

Q: You remember that you never flirted with the accused?

Q: You remember that you were not romantically interested in the accused?

Q: You are positive that you were not romantically interested in him because you had a boyfriend at the time?

Q: Your boyfriend's name was Cliff?

Q: Cliff was not at the club with you that night?

Q: He was at a fraternity party?

Q: The party was called a mixer?

Q: It is when fraternity boys and sorority girls get together for a party?

Q: You were not invited to the party?

Q: But, you were in a serious relationship with Cliff on the night in question?

Q: You remember dancing with your friend Julia?

Q: You remember dancing with your friend Julia for 4-5 songs?

Q: You have a vivid memory of only dancing with her?

Q: You don't remember dancing with the accused?

Q: You may have danced with him?

Q: You don't remember grinding into the accused?

Q: You may have grinded into him?

Q: You don't remember gyrating your hips into the accused's crotch?

Q: You may have gyrated your hips into him?

Q: You don't remember kissing the accused?

Q: You may have kissed him?

Q: You don't remember hugging the accused?

Q: You may have hugged him?

Q: You don't remember exchanging phone numbers with the accused?

Q: You may have exchanged numbers with him?

Q: You don't remember inviting the accused back to your dorm room?

Q: You may have invited him back to your dorm room?

Q: You don't remember texting the accused when you got back to the dorm?

Q: You may have texted him when you got back to the dorm?

Q: You don't remember opening the door for him?

Q: You may have opened the door for him?

Q: He didn't have a key to your room?

Q: You were alone in the room?

Q: You don't have a roommate?

Q: You have the only key to the room?

Q: You don't remember consenting to having sex with him?

Q: You may have consented to having sex with him?

Q: You don't remember performing oral sex on him?

Q: You may have performed oral sex on him?

Q: You don't remember him performing oral sex on you?

Q: He may have performed oral sex on you?

Q: You don't remember kissing him on your bed?

Q: You may have kissed him on your bed?

Q: You don't remember taking your pants off?

Q: You may have removed your pants?

Q: You don't remember taking your bra off?

Q: You may have taken off your bra?

Q: You don't remember taking your boots off?

Q: You may have taken off your boots?

Q: You don't remember taking your underwear off?

Q: You may have removed your underwear?

Point: Victim does not remember facts that make him/her look bad.

Q: You don't remember what happened after you left the club?

Q: But, you are positive that you did not invite the accused back to your dorm room?

Q: You don't remember what happened when you got to your dorm?

Q: But, you are positive that you did not open the door for him?

Q: You don't remember what happened in your dorm room?

Q: But, you are positive that you did not consent to having sex with him?

Q: You don't remember how your pants got off?

Q: But, you are positive that you did not take your pants off?

Q: You don't remember how your bra was removed?

Q: But, you are positive that you did not take your bra off?

Q: You don't remember how your underwear were removed?

Q: But, you are positive that you did not take your underwear off?

Q: You don't remember what type of sex occurred?

Q: But, you are positive that you did not perform oral sex on him?

Point: Bolstering the victim's memory.

Q: You clearly remember my client harassing you at the club?

Q: You have a vivid memory of walking out of the club?

Q: You clearly remember walking down those stairs?

Q: You have a vivid memory of walking to the car?

Q: You have a vivid memory of the ride to your dorm?

Q: You have a clear memory of what you talked about on the way to the dorm?

Q: But you don't remember _____?

Q: But you don't remember _____?

Point: Victim remembers sex but nothing leading up to it.

Q: Now, let's talk about what happened when you got to the room.

Q: You were in the room alone?

Q: You do not recall kissing the accused?

Q: You do not recall making out on your bed?

Q: You do not recall taking off your clothes?

Q: You do not recall touching the accused?

Q: You do not recall him kissing your breasts?

Q: The next thing you remember is the accused on top of you?

Q: Having sex with you?

Q: After that point, you can remember what happened?

Q: You remember what you did?

Q: You claim you pushed him?

Q: You claim you fought him?

Q: You remember what you said?

Q: You claim you said, "no?"

Q: You claim you screamed, "stop?"

Q: You remember telling the accused that you did not want sex?

Q: You remember telling the accused to leave your room?

Point: The victim claims she does not know how the accused got into her room.

Q: How did the accused get into your dorm room?

A: I don't know.

Q: You didn't let him in?

A: I did not let him in.

Q: You are positive that you did not open the door for him?

A: I would not have done that.

Q: You are positive that you did not invite him into the room?

A: Yes.

Q: Let's talk about how he could have gotten in?

A: Okay.

Q: He did not have a key, did he?

A: Not that I know of.

Q: You did not give him a key?

A: No.

Q: You never saw him with a key?

A: No.

Q: You only have one key to your door?

A: I guess.

Q: That key was on your keychain all night long?

A: I don't know.

Q: The only way into your room is the front door?

A: Yes.

Q: There is only one door?

A: Yes.

Q: The door has a lock that locks automatically?

A: Yes.

Q: When the door closes, it locks?

A: Yes.

Q: You don't have to turn the lock to lock it?

A: No.

Q: It locks even if you don't try to lock it?

A: Yes.

Q: It also has a dead bolt?

A: Yes.

Q: The dead bolt allows you to dead bolt the door from the inside?

A: Yes.

Q: Did he kick the door open?

A: I don't know.

Q: Did you hear anyone kicking the door?

A: No.

Q: You have been in the same dorm room since the alleged assault?

A: Yes.

Q: You have not noticed any damage to the door?

A: Not really.

Q: You have not noticed any damage to the door?

A: I didn't look?

Q: You have not noticed any damage to the door?

A: No.

Q: You have not noticed any damage to the doorframe?

A: No.

Q: You have not noticed any damage to the lock?

A: No.

Q: You have not noticed any damage to the door handle?

A: No.

Q: The police did not notice damage to the door?

A: I don't know.

Q: You didn't tell the police that you thought someone kicked your door in?

A: No.

Q: You didn't report any damage to the door?

A: No.

Q: He could not have climbed through the window?

A: I'm not sure. Anything is possible.

Q: It is possible that you opened the door and invited him in?

A: No, that didn't happen.

Q: Your room is on the 5th floor of the building?

A: Yeah.

Q: There is no balcony?

A: No.

Q: Unless he is Spider-Man, he did not come through the window?

A: I don't know?

Q: Your window was locked?

A: I don't remember.

Q: The window was not broken?

A: No.

Q: Have you ever witnessed anyone climb through one of these 5th floor windows?

A: No.

Q: Have you ever climbed out your window?

A: No.

Q: It is a 50 foot drop to the ground, from your window?

A: I don't know. I'm not good with numbers.

Q: You think you could jump out your window and survive the fall?

A: Never tried.

Q: You didn't report any damage to the window?

A: No.

Q: He could have walked through the wall, like a ghost?

A: I don't think so.

Q: Or, you could have let him in?

A: I didn't let him in?

CLOTHING REMOVAL

While an adult can be undressed while sleeping, and without waking up, it is unlikely unless the victim is drugged or heavily intoxicated. In some cases, the victim undresses herself or assists the accused in taking off her clothing. Then, consensual sexual activity occurs. Later, the victim claims the clothing was removed without consent, while she remained asleep. If the defense is *consent*, the cross examiner must question the victim about the type and fit of the clothing worn, and demonstrate that it is improbable she slept through the removal of all of her clothing, only to wake up as the sex was underway.

Point: Victim undressed while sleeping, but did not wake up.

Q: You testified that you went to bed fully clothed?

Q: When you woke up, you were undressed?

Q: You have no idea how your clothes were removed?

Q: You went to bed wearing skintight jeans?

Q: Skinny jeans they are called?

Q: The jeans went from your waist to your ankles?

Q: They were tight?

Q: They are skintight?

Q: They take a few minutes to put on?

Q: Even if you are perfectly sober, the jeans take time to put on?

Q: Because they are so tight?

Q: You cannot just slip off the jeans?

Q: When you are removing them, it takes effort?

Q: You did not feel anyone removing your pants?

Q: No tugging on them?

Q: No pulling on them?

Q: You claim that you were asleep while these jeans were being removed from your body?

Q: You were also wearing a shirt?

Q: You clearly remember wearing a shirt when you went to bed?

Q: It was long-sleeved?

Q: It was a tight sweater?

Q: When you woke up, you claim you were naked?

Q: You were wearing nothing?

Q: No pants?

Q: No shirt?

Q: No bra?

Q: No underwear?

Q: At the time of the alleged assault, you were 5' 7"?

Q: You weighed about 185 pounds?

CHAPTER 3: CROSS EXAMINING THE SEXUAL ASSAULT FORENSIC EXAMINER

GENERAL PURPOSE OF THE SEXUAL ASSAULT FORENSIC EXAM

This series of questions establishes the purpose of the sexual assault exam and the examiner's responsibilities.

Point: You carefully look for evidence so that it can be used by law enforcement?

Q: The purpose of the sexual assault exam is to collect evidence?

Q: The exam takes a few hours?

Q: The exam is deliberate?

Q: You carefully examine the entire body?

Q: You carefully record what you see?

Q: You carefully document evidence?

Q: If you see injuries, you take photos of the injuries?

Q: You preserve evidence so that it can be used by law enforcement?

COLLECTION AND PRESERVATION OF EVIDENCE

This series of questions establishes the examiner's duty to properly document and collect evidence to be used in a criminal trial.

Point: The sexual assault examiner is a vital link in the collection of evidence for the crime laboratory.

Q: Crime laboratories analyze evidence collected in sexual assault cases?

Q: Crime laboratories rely on medical examiners to collect and preserve evidence in sexual assault cases?

Q: Law enforcement rely on medical examiners to collect and preserve evidence in sexual assault cases?

Q: If evidence is not collected, then it cannot be examined?

Q: If evidence is not preserved, then it cannot be examined?

Q: As a sexual assault examiner, you play a vital role in the collection and preservation of evidence?

Q: The collection of evidence is one of your primary roles as a sexual assault forensics examiner?

EVIDENCE COLLECTION

In a sexual assault case, it is vital that sexual assault examiners recognize and properly collect evidence, whether the evidence is inculpatory or exculpatory. When cross-examining a sexual assault forensic examiner, the lawyer must highlight that it is crucial for the examiner to properly identify and collect evidence. The jury must understand that the failure to identify and collect evidence can make or break a case, and can cause serious doubt about what actually happened in the case.

Point: It is vital that examiners recognize and properly collect evidence.

Q: Sex assault examiners must know how to recognize potential evidence?

Q: Sex assault examiners must know how to collect evidence?

Q: Sex assault examiners must know how to preserve evidence?

Q: The evidence you collect may be sent to a forensics laboratory?

Q: The evidence you collect may be used in a criminal case?

Q: The proper collection of evidence is critical in a criminal case?

Q: The preservation of evidence is critical in a criminal case?

COLLECTION OF EVIDENCE: TIME FRAME GUIDELINES

In sexual assault cases, evidence should be collected and preserved as soon as possible; physical and forensic evidence is lost and degraded over time. The cross examiner must highlight these facts to the fact finder.

Point: Evidence is lost from the body over time; it is important to collect evidence in a timely manner.

Q: Now I want to talk to you about evidence in sexual assault cases?

Q: In a sexual assault case, evidence is lost from the body over time?

Q: Evidence is lost from clothing over time?

Q: It is important to collect evidence properly?

Q: It is important to collect evidence in a timely manner?

Q: Evidence should be collected as soon as possible to prevent it from being lost?

Q: Evidence should be collected as soon as possible to prevent it from being degraded?

DOCUMENTATION OF PHYSICAL INJURIES

In sexual assault cases where bleeding is noted, the examiner should document the source of the bleeding in their report. This fact is critical at trial; the source of the bleeding can help prove the guilt or innocence of the accused. Often, however, the examiner will note the presence of blood, but will not indicate the source. This can be misleading or confusing to the jury, who may associate the blood with an injury inflicted during the alleged crime, even if no injury exists. Blood can be attributed to a variety of sources that include, among other things, injury from consensual or non-consensual sex, a past or current menstruation, and certain methods of birth control.

Point: Source of vaginal bleeding should be documented.

....

Q: In your exam, you noted vaginal bleeding/spotting?

Q: In your report, it does not say what caused the bleeding?

Q: According to your training, when vaginal bleeding is found, the examiner should document the source of the bleeding?

Q: In this case, you were unable to determine the source of the bleeding?

Q: You did not see any cuts?

Q: You did not see any tears?

Q: You did not see any rips?

Q: If you had seen the source of the bleeding, you would have documented it?

Point: Vaginal bleeding/spotting can be caused by multiple sources.

....

Q: In your exam, you noted vaginal bleeding/spotting?

Q: In your report, it does not say what caused the bleeding?

Q: Blood can be attributed to a variety of sources?

Q: Blood can be attributed to an injury?

Q: Blood can be attributed to an injury caused by consensual sex?

Q: Blood can be attributed to an injury caused by non-consensual sex?

Q: Blood can be attributed to certain methods of birth control?

Q: Blood can be attributed to a current menstruation?

Q: Blood can be attributed to a past menstruation?

FORCED ORAL SODOMY CASES

In a sexual assault case involving an alleged forced oral sodomy, the examiner should carefully look for and document any injuries to the mouth. In violent oral sodomy cases, the mouth is commonly injured. If an alleged victim describes a violent oral assault, then the lack of injuries to the mouth are noteworthy, depending on the time elapsed from the assault to the examination.

If a victim describes a violent oral sodomy and they are examined within 24-48 hours, then the lack of oral injuries may cause doubt about the force used. The cross examiner must highlight to the jury that the examiner carefully looked for and documented any injuries to the mouth.

Point: Examiner documented injuries to the mouth.

Q: In this case, you examined the victim's mouth?

Q: You examined the mouth because she claimed that the accused forced his penis into her mouth?

Q: When there's an allegation of forced oral sodomy, you have been trained to look at the inside of the mouth?

Q: You have also been trained to look outside the mouth?

Q: When examining the mouth, you are looking for evidence?

Q: You are looking for injuries?

Q: You look for injuries to the lips?

Q: You look for injuries to the gums?

Q: You look for injuries to the soft and hard palate?

Q: You look for injuries to other parts of the mouth?

Q: You look for injuries such as bruising?

Q: You look for injuries such as cuts?

Q: You look for injuries such as redness?

Q: You look for injuries such as tears?

Q: You look for injuries such as lacerations?

Q: You look for anything out of the ordinary?

Q: In this case, you examined the outside of the mouth?

Q: In this case, you examined the inside of the mouth?

Q: In this case, you documented what you observed in and around the mouth?

Q: In your medical report, there is a section for oral or mouth injuries?

Q: You are required to document any injuries on your report?

Point: You found no injuries to the victim's mouth.

Q: Let's talk about what you wrote in your medical report in this case?

Q: You found no injuries inside the mouth?

Q: You found no injury on the outside of the mouth?

Q: You found no injury to the lips?

Q: You found no injury to the gums?

Q: You found no injury to the soft and hard palate?

Q: You found no injury to other parts of the mouth?

Q: You found no bruising?

Q: You found no cuts?

Q: You found no redness?

Q: You found no tears?

Q: You found no lacerations?

Q: Your medical report states that there were no injuries found in or around the mouth?

Point: No injuries to the mouth is consistent with consensual oral sex.

Q: When oral sex is consensual, you rarely see any lacerations to the mouth?

Q: When oral sex is consensual, you rarely see bruising of the mouth?

Q: When oral sex is consensual, you rarely see any cuts to the mouth?

Q: When oral sex is consensual, you rarely see any injuries to the mouth?

MOUTH INJURIES

If the examiner finds mouth injuries, it does not necessarily mean they were caused by non-consensual sex. Consensual sexual activity can cause injury to the mouth. The injuries depend on the type of sex, the force used, and whether other objects were inserted into the mouth. The cross examiner must explore the potential causes of the injuries.

Point: Consensual oral sex can injure the mouth.

Q: Consensual oral sex can cause swelling to the inside of the mouth?

Q: Consensual oral sex can cause bruising to the mouth?

Q: Consensual oral sex can cause redness to the mouth?

Q: Consensual oral sex can cause injury to the soft palate?

Q: Consensual oral sex can cause injury to the hard palate?

Q: Consensual oral sex can cause injuries?

Q: Mouth injuries depend on various factors?

Q: They can depend on the length of the oral sex?

Q: They can depend on the type of oral sex?

Q: They depend on the size of the penis?

Q: They depend on how deep the penis went into the mouth?

Q: They depend on the force used?

Q: Some people, when performing oral sex, like to "deep throat" the penis?

Q: They can also depend on how experienced the person performing oral sex was at performing oral sex?

Point: Sex toys can injure the mouth.

Q: Sex toys can cause swelling to the inside of the mouth?

Q: Sex toys can cause bruising to the mouth?

Q: Sex toys can cause redness to the mouth?

Q: Sex toys can cause injury to the soft palate?

Q: Sex toys can cause injury to the hard palate?

Q: Sex toys can cause various injuries?

Q: Mouth injuries depend on various factors?

Q: It depends on how deep the object went into the mouth?

Q: It depends on the force used?

Point: Ball gags can injure the mouth.

Q: Sex toys can cause various injuries?

Q: A ball gag is a sex toy?

Q: A ball gag is used in bondage?

Q: A ball gag is a sex toy that is placed inside a person's mouth?

Q: A ball gag consists of a ball on a rope that is shoved into the victim's mouth and tied tight?

Q: The purpose of a ball gag is so the person with the gag can't scream or say anything?

Q: A ball gag can cause swelling to the inside of the mouth?

Q: A ball gag can cause bruising to the mouth?

Q: A ball gag can cause redness to the mouth?

Q: A ball gag can cause injury to the soft palate?

Q: A ball gag can cause injury to the hard palate?

Q: Ball gag injuries depend on various factors?

Q: It depends on how tight the gag was tied?

Q: The tighter, the more likely there will be injury?

Q: It depends on the size of the ball gag?

Q: It depends on various other factors?

Q: Such as how hard the gagged person was biting on the ball?

Point: Rough consensual oral sex can injure the mouth.

Q: Rough consensual oral sex can cause swelling to the inside of the mouth?

Q: Rough consensual oral sex can cause bruising to the mouth?

Q: Rough consensual oral sex can cause redness to the mouth?

Q: Rough consensual oral sex can cause injury to the soft palate?

Q: Rough consensual oral sex can cause injury to the hard palate?

Q: Rough consensual oral sex can cause injuries?

Q: Mouth injuries depend on various factors?

Q: They depend on the length of time the oral sex is performed?

Q: They depend on the type of oral sex?

Q: It depends on the size of the penis?

Q: It depends on how deep the penis went into the mouth?

Q: It depends on the force used?

Q: Some people, when performing oral sex, like to "deep throat" the penis?

Q: It depends on how experienced the person, who was performing oral sex, was at performing oral sex?

ANAL INJURIES

In cases involving both consensual and nonconsensual anal sex, it is common to find anal injury. The cross examiner must show the jury that injury to the anus does not mean the sex was nonconsensual.

Point: Consensual anal intercourse can injure the anus.

Q: Anal intercourse can cause injuries to the anus?

Q: According to medical literature/your training, 50% of those who engage in anal intercourse have evident injury afterwards?

Q: However, serious injury is rare?

Q: Serious injuries are rare because the anus and anal canal can expand?

Q: The amount of lubrication used makes a difference in anal injuries?

Q: Lots of lubrication can help avoid injury?

Q: The less lubrication used, the more likely the injury?

Q: Consensual anal sex can cause tears in the anus?

Q: Consensual anal sex can cause rips?

Q: Consensual anal sex can cause redness?

Q: Consensual anal sex can cause swelling?

Q: Consensual anal sex can cause injuries?

NON-GENITAL INJURIES IN SEXUAL ASSAULT CASES

Point: Non-genital injuries are common in a sexual assault.

Q: During your exam, you looked for non-genital injuries?

Q: Non-genital injuries are injuries to other parts of the body aside from the genitalia?

Q: The genitals would include the penis and vagina?

Q: An example of a non-genital injury, would be scratches on the arm?

Q: Another example of a non-genital injury, would be a bruise on the wrist?

Q: Or a bruise on the neck?

Q: Non-genital injuries sometimes occur in sexual assault cases?

Q: Non-genital injuries can be caused by force?

Q: Non-genital injuries can be caused by violence?

Q: For example, if a person was violently raped, you may find non-genital injuries on their body?

Point: Non-genital injuries can occur in consensual sex.

Q: Non-genital injuries can occur in consensual sex?

Q: Non-genital injuries such as scratches can occur in consensual sex?

Q: Non-genital injuries such as bruising can occur in consensual sex?

Q: Non-genital injuries can occur when people engage in rough sex?

Point: Sexual assault can cause non-genital injuries.

Q: Sexual offenders have been known to use force during an attack?

Q: Sexual offenders have been known to use violence during an attack?

Q: When violence is used, sometimes the victim is bruised?

Q: When violence is used, sometimes the victim gets abrasions on the body?

Q: When violence is used, sometimes the victim gets lacerations on the body?

Q: Bruising, abrasions, and lacerations on the body could indicate a struggle occurred?

Q: That is why you examine the entire body of the victim?

Point: You carefully documented all non-genital injuries.

Q: When you look for non-genital injuries, you look carefully?

Q: When you look for non-genital injuries, you are deliberate?

Q: You examine the victim from head to toe?

Q: You examine the victim while the victim is naked?

Q: You examine the body without clothes on so that no part is obstructed from view?

Q: You document all injuries that you find?

Q: Non-genital trauma sometimes occurs during a sex assault?

Q: During your examination, you looked at the victim's neck?

Q: You looked at/behind the victim's ears?

Q: You looked at the victim's wrists?

Q: You looked at other parts of the body?

Q: If you see an injury, you write it in your report?

Q: You document the size of the injury?

Q: You document the location of the injury?

Q: You describe the injury in your report?

Q: You also photograph the injury?

EAR INJURIES

Point: Ear injuries occur in sexual assault.

Q: In sexual assault cases, you look behind the ears for injuries?

Q: You are looking for bruising and swelling of the tissue around the mastoid bone?

Q: The mastoid bone is behind the ears?

Q: Injury behind the ears is common when a perpetrator holds a victim for sexual intercourse?

Q: These injuries are called clapping injuries?

Q: They are caused by someone physically restraining the victim?

Point: No ear injuries were documented.

Q: In this case, you did not observe any injuries to the ears?

Q: In this case, you did not observe any injuries behind the ears?

Q: Your report does not mention any injuries to the ears?

Q: Your report does not mention any injuries behind the ears?

Q: If you found injuries to the ears, they would have been in your report?

Q: You would have taken photographs?

WRIST INJURIES

Point: Wrist injuries occur in sexual assault.

Q: In sexual assault cases, you look for injuries on the victim's wrists?

Q: Wrists can be bruised when a perpetrator holds the victim's wrists?

Q: Wrists are commonly bruised when a perpetrator forcefully holds the victim's wrists?

Point: No wrist injuries were documented.

Q: In this case, you did not observe any injuries to the wrists?

Q: Your report does not mention any injuries to the wrists?

Q: If you found injuries to the wrists, they would have been in your report?

Q: You would have taken photographs?

NECK INJURIES

Point: Neck injuries occur in sexual assault.

Q: In sexual assault cases, you look for injuries on the victim's neck?

Q: The neck can be bruised when a perpetrator chokes the victim?

Q: The neck can be bruised when a perpetrator grabs the victim's neck or throat?

Q: The neck can be bruised when a perpetrator strangles the victim?

Q: The neck is commonly bruised when a perpetrator forcefully holds the victim's neck or throat?

Q: The neck can be bruised when a perpetrator bites the victim?

Q: The neck can be bruised when a perpetrator scratches the victim?

Point: No neck injuries were documented.

Q: In this case, you did not observe any injuries to the neck or throat?

Q: Your report does not mention any injuries to the neck?

Q: If you found injuries on the neck, they would have been in your report?

Q: You would have taken photographs?

SMOTHERING INJURIES

Point: Smothering can cause injuries.

Q: In smothering cases, injuries are commonly found around the victim's mouth?

Q: In smothering cases, injuries are commonly found around the victim's nose?

Q: This occurs when the assailant's hand presses into the mouth and nose?

Q: The victim's teeth can also cause injuries to the victim's mouth and lips when smothered?

Point: You documented no smothering injuries.

Q: In this case, you did not observe any injuries to the victim's mouth?

Q: In this case, you did not observe any injuries to the victim's nose?

Q: Your report does not mention any injuries to the mouth or nose?

Q: If you had found injuries on the mouth or nose, they would have been in your report?

Q: You would have taken photographs?

INJURIES TO THE ASSAILANT

Note: In sexual assault cases, a forensic examiner often physically examines the suspected assailant. The injuries or lack of injuries to the suspect's body can help to prove or disprove that an assault occurred. Injuries or a lack of injuries can help the fact finder make a more informed decision.

Point: Assailants are often injured during a sexual assault.

Q: In violent sexual assaults, the assailant is sometimes scratched?

Q: In violent sexual assaults, the assailant is sometimes hit?

Q: In violent sexual assaults, the assailant is sometimes bitten?

Q: In violent sexual assaults, the assailant is sometimes kneed?

Q: In violent sexual assaults, the assailant is sometimes injured during the struggle?

Q: Injuries on the face of the assailant can indicate a struggle?

Q: Injuries on the body of the assailant can indicate a struggle?

Point: You carefully examined the assailant for injuries.

Q: In this case, you examined the accused?

Q: You were looking for injuries to the accused's body?

Q: You looked at the accused's face?

Q: You looked at the accused's neck?

Q: You looked at the accused's chest?

Q: You looked at the accused's shoulders?

Q: You looked at the accused's back?

Q: You looked at the accused's arms?

Q: You looked at the accused's penis?

Q: You looked at the accused's fingernails?

Q: You looked at his entire body?

Q: You were looking for injuries to the accused's body that would show a struggle?

Q: You were looking for injuries such as scratches?

Q: You were looking for bite marks?

Q: You were looking for cuts?

Q: You were looking for abrasions?

Q: You were looking for bruises?

Q: You were looking for redness?

Q: You were looking for lacerations?

Q: You were looking for swelling?

Point: You documented no injuries to the suspected assailant.

Q: In this case, you did not observe any injuries to the accused's face?

Q: You did not observe any injuries to the accused's neck?

Q: You did not observe any injuries to the accused's chest?

Q: You did not observe any injuries to the accused's shoulders?

Q: You did not observe any injuries to the accused's back?

Q: You did not observe any injuries to the accused's arms?

Q: You did not observe any injuries to the accused's penis?

Q: You did not observe any injuries to the accused's fingernails?

Q: You did not observe any scratches on the accused?

Q: You did not observe any bite marks on the accused?

Q: You did not observe any cuts on the accused?

Q: You did not observe any abrasions on the accused?

Q: You did not observe any bruises on the accused?

Q: You did not observe any redness on the accused?

Q: You did not observe any lacerations on the accused?

Q You did not observe any swelling on the accused?

Q: Your report mentions no injuries to the accused?

Q: In this case, you did not observe any injuries on the accused's body?

Q: If you found injuries, they would have been in your report?

Q: You would have taken photographs?

CONSENSUAL SEX INJURIES

When the victim has genital injuries, the prosecution will likely argue that such injuries are "consistent" with a sexual assault. However, the injuries may also be consistent with consensual sexual activity. The cross examiner must show the jury that both consensual and nonconsensual sex can cause genital injuries. Otherwise, the fact finder may conclude that the injuries must have been cause by lack of consent.

Point: Injuries sometimes occur in consensual intercourse.

Q: Injuries sometimes occur during consensual intercourse?

Q: When a husband and wife have consensual sex, there can be genital injuries afterwards?

Q: The types of injuries in consensual sex are similar to those during nonconsensual intercourse?

Q: The types of injuries in consensual sex are often the same as in nonconsensual intercourse?

Q: After consensual sex, there may be abrasions?

Q: After consensual sex, there may be redness?

Q: After consensual sex, there may be swelling?

Q: After consensual sex, there may be bruising?

Q: After consensual sex, there may be tears?

Q: After consensual sex, there may be micro-tears?

Point: The human body is designed to cause minimal injuries during sex.

Q: The human body is designed to prevent injuries during sex?

Q: For example, the body lubricates itself to facilitate sex?

Q: Some women present more lubrication than others?

Q: The amount of lubrication depends on various factors?

Q: Certain medical conditions can affect the amount of lubrication?

Q: Certain medicines can affect the amount of lubrication?

Q: The amount of lubrication can vary depending on the stage of the menstrual cycle?

Point: Injury locations are similar in consensual and non-consensual sex.

Q: The locations of injuries are often the same in consensual and non-consensual sex?

Q: The posterior fourchette is commonly injured during consensual intercourse?

Q: Hypervascularity is a common finding in females after engaging in consensual intercourse?

Q: The labia menora is commonly injured during consensual intercourse?

Q: The hymen is commonly injured during consensual intercourse?

Q: The fossa novicularis is commonly injured during consensual intercourse?

Q: Consent does not preclude trauma in adults?

Point: Adolescents aged 12 to 18 have a higher rate of injury in consensual sex.

Q: Now I want to discuss injuries in adolescents, understood?

Q: An adolescent is someone between the ages of 12 and 18?

Q: The alleged victim in this case was an adolescent?

Q: You found injuries to the victim in this case?

Q: In adolescents aged 12 to 18, the chance of perineal lacerations from nonconsensual sex was similar to that of those engaging in consensual sex?

Q: In other words, adolescents engaged in consensual sex can get lacerations?

Q: Consent does not preclude trauma in adolescents?

Point: Human bodies naturally prepare for sex.

Q: Now I want to talk about the human sexual response, okay?

Q: Human bodies naturally prepare for sex?

Q: This is called the human sexual response?

Q: For example, with males, the penis becomes erect?

Q: The penis becomes erect in preparation for sexual intercourse?

Q: With the female, one thing the body does is lubricate itself?

Point: Pelvic tilt occurs in consensual sex.

Q: I want to talk about pelvic tilt, okay?

Q: Pelvic tilt is when the female tilts her hips?

Q: If on her back, she tilts the hips upwards, towards the man on top?

Q: This allows the penis to more easily enter the vagina?

Q: This is part of the human sexual response?

Q: In other words, this is how humans are designed to have sex?

Q: And reproduce?

Q: The pelvic tilt helps to prevent injuries?

Q: Pelvic tilt is a conscious decision?

Q: Pelvic tilt usually occurs in consensual sex?

Point: Partner assistance with insertion occurs in consensual sex.

Q: I want to talk about partner assistance with insertion, okay?

Q: Partner assistance is when the female helps insert the penis into her vagina?

Q: She helps guide it in?

Q: This allows the penis to more easily enter the vagina?

Q: Partner assistance helps to prevent injuries?

Q: Partner assistance is a conscious decision?

Q: Partner assistance occurs in consensual sex?

Point: A non-relaxed victim is more likely to be injured.

Q: I want to talk about relaxation by the female during sex, okay?

Q: The woman's level of relaxation plays a role in the amount, if any, of injuries to the vagina?

Q: During sex, the more relaxed a woman is, the less trauma that occurs?

Q: If the woman is tense, her vagina may be more tense?

Q: It is easier for a penis to penetrate a relaxed vagina?

Q: Relaxation is part of the human sexual response?

Q: Relaxation by the woman helps to prevent injuries?

Point: The human sexual response may reduce injuries.

Q: Pelvic tilt helps reduce injuries?

Q: Increased vaginal lubrication helps reduce injuries?

Q: Partner assistance with insertion helps reduce injuries?

Q: Relaxation helps reduce injuries?

Q: In this case, there was supposedly no pelvic tilt?

Q: In this case, there was supposedly no partner assistance with insertion?

Q: In this case, there was supposedly no increase in lubrication?

Q: In this case, there was supposedly no relaxation?

Point: A person in fear is not relaxed.

Q: A person in fear is usually tense?

Q: A person in fear is not relaxed?

Q: A person in a physical altercation is usually not relaxed?

Q: Here, the alleged victim claimed to have been scared?

Q: Here, the alleged victim claimed to have been terrified?

Q: Here, the alleged victim claimed to have been in fear for her life?

Q: Here, the alleged victim claimed to have been resisting the assault?

Q: Here, the alleged victim claimed to have been fighting off the assault?

Q: Here, the alleged victim claimed to have been trying to get away?

Q: Here, the alleged victim claimed to have been struggling?

Point: A person being sexually assaulted usually does not naturally prepare for sex.

Q: The normal sexual response is typically absent in the victim during a sexual assault?

Q: In a violent rape there is no pelvic tilt?

Q: In a violent rape there is no partner assistance with insertion?

Q: In a violent rape there is no increase in lubrication?

Q: In a violent rape there is no relaxation?

Q: In this case, the victim said she was resisting?

Q: She said she was fighting?

Q: She said she was struggling?

Q: She said she was not relaxing?

Q: She said she was not helping him insert his penis?

THE STAGES OF HUMAN SEXUAL RESPONSE

Point: A stimulated body prepares for sexual intercourse.

Q: Now let's talk about the stages or phases of the human sexual response in women, okay?

Q: When a person is sexually stimulated, their body goes through changes?

Q: Their body prepares for sexual intercourse?

Q: The first stage is excitement?

Q: This is when the body reacts to physical or psychological stimulation?

Q: In other words, the female becomes excited or turned on?

Q: This first stage involves the vaginal walls lubricating?

Q: The second phase of human sexual response is the plateau?

Q: In the plateau sexual tension intensifies?

Q: In this phase, the uterus elevates and tilts back?

Q: The fundus contracts to form a reservoir for sperm?

Q: In this phase, the vagina extends from an average of 2 cm wide by 7.5 cm long to 5.75 cm wide and 10.5 cm long?

Q: During this phase, the vagina is tenable to accommodate the delivery of the penis head?

Q: During this phase, the labia minora becomes larger?

GENITAL INJURIES

Point: Tampons and other objects can cause genital injury.

Q: Plastic applicators encasing the tampon may cause lacerations?

Q: Inserting tampons can also cause mechanical erosion?

Q: Fingers and fingernails can cause injuries to the vagina?

Q: Other foreign objects can cause genital injury?

Q: A speculum can cause genital injury?

Point: Genital injuries may be caused by various factors.

Q: Pelvic tilt is when the female adjusts her pelvis to allow easier insertion of the penis?

Q: Lack of pelvic tilt could cause an injury?

Q: Lack of lubrication could cause an injury?

Q: When the female is not relaxed, this could also lead to injury?

Q: Lack of partner assistance with insertion could cause an injury?

Q: By partner assistance, I mean when the partner helps insert the penis into the vagina?

Q: If you combine lack of pelvic tilt, lack of lubrication, and no partner assistance, the chances of an injury are higher?

Q: If there is pelvic tilt, partner assistance, and lubrication, then chances of an injury are less likely?

Q: Also, the size of the penis can make a difference?

Q: A large penis can sometimes cause additional injuries?

Point: Posterior fourchette is commonly injured during sex.

Q: In the missionary style position, where the female is on her back, the most common injuries are to:

Q: The posterior fourchette?

Q: The labia minor?

Q: The hymen?

Q: The fossa novicularis?

Q: And of these, the posterior fourchette is the most commonly injured?

Q: These areas can be injured during consensual sex as well?

LUBRICATION

Point: Lack of lubrication can cause abrasions.

Q: Lack of lubrication can cause abrasions?

Q: Lack of lubrication can cause lacerations?

Q: It is friction between the penis and the vagina that causes the abrasions or lacerations?

Q: It happens because the penis pushes inward and causes friction to the female organs?

Point: Injuries can occur when there is lubrication.

Q: Vaginal lacerations can occur even when there is sufficient lubrication?

Q: Ecchymosis or bruising can occur even when there is sufficient lubrication?

Q: Lubrication alone does not protect the genitalia from injury?

Q: Menstrual blood alone does not protect the genitalia from injury from non-consensual contact?

Point: A non-cooperating victim can result in more injuries.

Q: When the female is not cooperating, the penis can cause more blunt force trauma?

Q: When the female is not relaxing, the penis can cause blunt force trauma?

Q: This happens because the vagina is more rigid and less flexible?

Q: The more rigid the vagina, the more likely it will be injured?

FORCE OR VIOLENCE

Point: Force and violence increases risk of injury.

Q: The more force used against a victim, the higher the probability of injury?

Q: The more violence used against a victim, the higher the probability of injury?

Q: All sexual intercourse requires some level of force?

Q: Without some force, a penis could not enter into a vagina?

Point: Friction causes to injuries.

Q: Various factors can cause a lack of lubrication?

Q: Sexual dysfunction can cause a lack of lubrication?

Q: Some women produce more lubrication than others?

Q: Some women produce different levels of lubrication at different times of their menstrual cycle?

Q: Consensual sex can occur even when there is reduced lubrication?

Q: Prolonged sex can reduce lubrication?

Q: Repeated sex can cause a lack of lubrication?

Q: Repeated sex can cause injuries?

Q: One cause of repeated prolonged sex is delayed ejaculation?

Q: In other words, the sex takes longer because the male has trouble ejaculating?

Q: Reduced lubrication can prolong the time required to ejaculate?

Q: Reduced lubrication can increase trauma to the penis?

Q: Reduced lubrication can increase trauma to the vagina?

Q: Increased friction can increase trauma to the penis?

Q: Increased friction can increase trauma to the vagina?

Q: Reduced lubrication can increase the probability of injury?

Q: This is true even when the sex was consensual?

Q: Consensual sex can cause vaginal injuries?

PHYSICAL INJURY OR LACK THEREOF DOES NOT PROVE RAPE

Point: Lack of physical injuries does not prove sexual assault.

Q: The absence of genital injury in an alleged sexual assault victim can be explained by various factors:

Q: The lack of vaginal contact by the accused?

Q: Delayed reporting?

Q: The lack of magnification?

Q: The lack of training or experience by the examiner?

Q: A nonaggressive perpetrator?

Q: A non-resistive victim?

Q: False allegation?

Q: If the perpetrator had no contact with the vagina, then you would not expect to see genital injury?

Point: A sexual assault examiner must remain unbiased.

Q: Your task as an expert is to present information to help the jury understand specific patient evidence?

Q: This is done by providing qualified opinions?

Q: This is done by providing unbiased opinions?

Q: Let's talk about what it means to be unbiased, okay?

Q: It means your opinions should be scientifically sound?

Q: It means your testimony should be scientifically sound?

Q: It is not the goal of an examiner to act as an advocate for one side or the other?

Q: This is something you were trained on when you went through your training?

Q: As a medical professional your job is to treat the patient?

Q: And to collect evidence?

Q: You are taught that when you become an advocate, your testimony becomes suspect?

Q: You were taught that your credibility as an expert can be affected by whether or not you have a bias?

Q: Your job is to present facts in a neutral manner?

Q: In your training, you are taught to review related scientific literature prior to testifying?

Q: You are taught to keep reference materials and relevant articles that deal with the topics about which you were testifying about?

Point: Vaginal abrasions can be caused by various things.

Q: You mentioned that you found an abrasion in the vagina?

Q: An abrasion means that skin or mucous membrane is removed?

Q: Many things can cause an abrasion to the vaginal area?

Q: Sexual intercourse can cause abrasions to the vagina?

Q: Consensual sex can cause an abrasion to the vaginal area?

Q: Consensual sex between a husband and wife can cause a vaginal abrasion?

Q: Consensual sex between a boyfriend and girlfriend can cause a vaginal abrasion?

Q: It is documented in medial literature that vaginal injuries often occur in consensual sex?

Q: A penis can cause a vaginal abrasion?

Q: A sex toy can cause a vaginal abrasion?

Q: A speculum can cause a vaginal abrasion?

Q: What is a speculum?

Q: Fingers can cause an abrasion to the vaginal area?

Q: Fingernails can cause an abrasion to the vaginal area?

Q: A tampon can cause an abrasion to the vaginal area?

Q: Inserting birth control can cause an abrasion to the vaginal area?

Q: If a woman uses her fingers to stimulate her vagina, it can cause an abrasion?

Q: If a man consensually uses his fingers to stimulate a woman's vagina, it can cause an abrasion?

Q: You were not present when the abrasion occurred?

Q: You cannot tell what exact time and date the abrasion occurred?

Q: You did not see what caused the injury?

Point: Some vaginal injuries are microscopic.

Q: Sometimes vaginal abrasions are microscopic?

Q: Many abrasions cannot be seen with the naked eye?

Q: Sometimes abrasions are microscopic?

Q: For example, my hand could have an abrasion you would not be able to see if you looked at it right now?

Q: When you conduct a sexual assault forensic exam, you look at the vagina?

Q: This is called a visual inspection?

Q: You make sure the vagina is well lit?

Q: You do that so you can clearly see visible injuries?

Point: You examined the entire body and documented all injuries.

Q: You examined the entire body looking for injuries and documented all injuries?

Q: You looked at the patient from head to toe?

Q: You documented bruises?

Q: You documented cuts?

Q: You documented tears?

Q: You documented scrapes?

Q: You documented fingernail marks?

Q: You documented bite marks?

Q: You documented abrasions?

Q: You documented anything that could be an injury?

Q: You documented anything that was abnormal?

Q: You documented your findings on page (insert page number) of the sexual assault report?

Q: All injuries you found were required to be documented on this form?

Q: All injuries you found were required to be photographed?

Q: When you find an injury, you measure it?

Q: You describe its shape?

Q: You describe its color?

Q: You describe its details?

Q: In this case, you documented no injuries?

Point: You are required to note the location of any injury.

Q: On the sexual assault exam report there is an anatomical diagram of a female body?

Q: This diagram shows the front and back of the female body?

Q: The purpose of this diagram is for you to document the location of the injuries found?

Q: You are looking for ALL injuries, whether they came from the alleged assault or not?

Q: You document them all and send the medical records to the investigators and lawyers?

Q: In this case, according to your report, you found no injuries to the victim's body?

NO INJURIES FOUND ON THE BODY

The fact that no injuries were found on the victim's body after an allegedly violent struggle may be relevant in certain cases. If the forensic examination is done within 48 hours of the alleged assault, and the victim describes biting, scratching, hitting, and other violence, then the lack of injuries may cause doubt about the extent, if any, of the struggle.

While the lack of injuries on an alleged victim does not disprove that a crime occurred, it can help cast doubt on the allegations, depending on the facts of the case.

Point: You found no injuries after a violent struggle.

Q: In this case, I want to talk about what injuries you found during the full body exam, okay?

Q: You did a head to toe exam?

Q: When you carefully observed the alleged victim from head to toe, you found no scratches?

Q: You found no cuts?

Q: You found no bruises?

Q: You found no swelling?

Q: You found no redness?

Q: You found no abrasions?

Q: You found no fingernail marks?

Q: You found no tears?

Q: After a careful head to toe examination, you found no injuries whatsoever?

Q: That is what you documented on the SANE exam?

Q: That no injuries were found in the head to toe examination?

Q: If there are injuries, then you are required to document them?

Q: In this case, you did not document any injuries?

TEARS: TEARS, ECCHYMOSIS, ABRASION, REDNESS, SWELLING

Point: Injuries can be represented by the acronym TEARS.

Q: In sexual assault cases, there are five typical injury types?

Q: The types of injuries are easy to remember using the acronym TEARS?

Q: T stands for tears or lacerations?

Q: A tear is similar to a laceration or cut?

Q: E stands for ecchymosis or bruising?

Q: Ecchymosis is like bruising?

Q: A stands for abrasion?

Q: R stands for redness?

Q: S stands for swelling?

Point: The most commonly injured area in the female genitalia during missionary style sex is the posterior fourchette.

Q: The most commonly injured area in the female genitalia during missionary style sex is the posterior fourchette?

Q: This injury is commonly seen at the 5 to 7 o'clock position?

Q: This is common because this is where the penis first contacts the female genitalia?

Point: Your exam noted no injury to the patient.

Q: Let's talk about your report, page _____?

Q: This page asks you to diagram or draw the injuries you observed?

Q: You use that diagram to chart any injuries you observe?

Q: You examined the patient's labia majora and found no injury?

Q: You examined her labia minora and found no injury?

Q: You examined her perineum and found no injury?

Q: You examined her clitoris and found no injury?

Q: You examined her urethra and found no injury?

Q: You examined her hymen and found no injury?

Q: You examined her vagina and found no injury?

Q: In the medical report, you wrote, "no injury noted," correct?

Q: You wrote, "no injury noted," because you did not observe any injuries?

Point: You didn't look at the victim's vagina.

Q: You didn't look at her vagina, did you?

Q: You didn't look at the vagina because the patient told you there was no injury to the vagina?

Q: So you found no evidence of trauma to the patient's female sex organ?

Point: You found no injury to the patient's anus.

Q: You examined the patient's anus?

Q: The patient gave no history or information involving the anus?

Q: You did not expect to find any injury there?

Q: You did not find any injury to the patient's anus?

FRIABILITY AND LABIAL ADHESIONS IN CHILDREN

Point: Labial adhesions tend to bleed abnormally easily.

Q: Friability is a term used to describe tissues that bleed abnormally easily?

Q: For example, labial adhesions tend to bleed abnormally easily?

Q: A labial adhesion is a common disorder in females who have not reached puberty?

Q: A labial adhesion occurs when the labia minora is fused or connected in the midline?

Q: The adhesion or fusion of the surfaces may occur at any point along the labia?

Q: This occurs naturally?

Q: This can typically be treated conservatively?

Q: When the labial adhesion is gently separated, it often bleeds?

Q: A labial adhesion is commonly found in infants and young children?

(Note: It is unusual to appear for the first time after 6 to 7 years of age. May be related to chronic irritation. Also called labial agglutination.)

Q: The proper collection of evidence is crucial in the prosecution of sexual assault cases?

Q: Some cases rise and fall based on physical evidence?

Q: Some cases rise and fall based on forensic evidence?

Q: Some cases rise and fall based on scientific evidence?

MEDICAL HISTORY

Point: Examiner must obtain patient's forensic medical history.

Q: Now I want to discuss the forensic medical history you request from the patient, understood?

Q: The following information should be routinely sought from patients:

Q: The date and time of the alleged sexual assault(s)?

Q: It is essential to know the time that passed between the assault and the physical examination?

Q: It is important to know the time that passed between the assault and the collection of evidence?

Q: For example, some evidence does not appear immediately on the body?

Q: Bruising does not appear immediately on the body?

Q: Bruises change in their appearance over time?

Q: Some evidence disappears from the body over time?

Q: Wounds heal over time?

Q: DNA evidence is lost over time?

Q: The time between the assault and the documentation of injuries can affect the outcome of a case?

Point: Examiner must obtain patient medical history.

Q: An examiner must collect medical information about the patient being examined?

Q: The patient's menstrual history should be noted?

Q: The patient's menstrual history can affect the interpretation of the exam results?

Q: Blood found could be from a menstrual cycle?

Q: Recent anal or genital injuries should be noted in the report?

Q: Recent anal or genital injuries can affect the interpretation of the exam results?

Q: The patient's birth control can affect the interpretation of the exam results?

Q: Some forms of birth control cause spotting, or vaginal bleeding?

Q: A patient's past surgeries can affect the interpretation of the exam results?

Q: A patient's history of blood clotting can affect the interpretation of the exam results?

Point: Examiner must obtain patient's recent sexual history.

Q: An examiner must ask the patient about their recent sexual history?

Q: The sensitivity of DNA analysis makes it important to gather information about recent intercourse?

Q: You must gather information about recent anal, vaginal, and/or oral intercourse?

Q: You must also ask whether the prior sex involved a condom?

Q: You do this because semen may be found during your exam?

Q: The semen could belong to someone other than the accused?

Q: Other bodily fluids could also be found during the exam (saliva, blood, etc.)?

Q: But it might belong to someone other than the accused?

Q: You might also find genital injuries during your exam?

Q: But these injuries may not have been caused by the accused?

Q: That is why you ask about the patient's recent sexual history?

Q: Fluids or injuries that you find could have been from a prior sexual partner?

Q: That is why you ask about the patient's recent sexual history?

Point: Examiner must document patient's post-assault activities.

Q: An examiner must ask about the patient's post-assault activities?

Q: You ask about activities such as washing, changing clothes, eating, brushing teeth?

Q: It is critical to know what, if any, activities were performed before the examination?

Q: The quantity and quality of evidence can be affected by patient activities?

Q: An activity, such as brushing the teeth, could affect the quantity of evidence?

Q: An activity, such as taking a shower, could affect the quality of evidence?

Point: Examiner must ask if the patient is injured.

Q: An examiner must ask the patient about the assault?

Q: You ask the patient to describe what happened?

Q: You document what the patient tells you?

Q: For example, you ask about whether force was used?

Q: You ask about injuries?

Q: You ask where the injuries are located?

Q: You ask whether there is tenderness?

Q: Whether there is pain and/or bleeding?

Q: You ask whether there is tenderness to the anal and genital injury(s)?

Point: Examiner must ask the patient about the nature of the assault.

Q: As an examiner, you must ask the patient to describe the physical assault?

Q: You ask about the physical surroundings of the assault?

Q: You ask about the tactics employed by the suspect?

Q: The tactics used by the suspect are crucial to the detection, collection, and analysis of physical evidence?

Q: Tactics may include the use of weapons?

Q: Tactics may include physical blows?

Q: Tactics may include grabbing?

Q: Tactics may include holding?

Q: Tactics may include pinching?

Q: Tactics may include choking?

Q: Tactics may include biting?

Q: Tactics may include using physical restraints?

Q: Tactics may include strangulation?

Q: Tactics may include burns?

Q: Tactics may include threats of harm?

Q: Tactics may include involuntary ingestion of alcohol/drugs?

Point: The examiner must ask the patient if the suspect is injured.

Q: As an examiner, you ask the patient if the suspect could be injured?

Q: Knowing if the suspect is injured may be useful when recovering evidence from the patient?

Q: Knowing if the suspect is injured may be useful when recovering evidence from the suspect?

Q: A victim may describe scratching the suspect?

Q: So you ask about scratch marks?

Q: You can also collect fingernail scraping from the patient?

Q: You do this to determine whether the patient may have the suspect's DNA under his/her fingernails?

Q: You can also look for scratch marks or scars on the suspect?

Q: A victim may describe hitting the suspect in the face?

Q: You can look for bruises on the suspect's face?

Q: A victim may describe biting the suspect?

Q: The suspect's DNA may be recovered from the patient's mouth?

Q: Bite marks may be visible on the suspect?

Point: An examiner must ask whether drugs or alcohol were involved in the assault.

Q: As an examiner, you ask the patient if drugs or alcohol were involved in the assault?

Q: This is called an alcohol or drug-facilitated sexual assault?

Q: The examiner should look for the presence of drugs and alcohol in the patient?

Q: It is critical in alcohol or drug-facilitated sexual assault cases to ask if the patient suffered memory loss?

Q: It is important to ask if the patient had a lapse of consciousness?

Q: It is important to ask if the patient vomited?

Q: It is important to ask if the patient was given food or drink by the suspect?

Q: It is important to ask if the patient voluntarily ingested drugs or alcohol?

Q: When possible, toxicology samples should be collected within 120 hours of alleged ingestion?

Point: An examiner must get an accurate description of the assault.

Q: As an examiner, you must get an accurate description of the sexual assault from the patient?

Q: The patient's version of the sexual assault is crucial to detecting, collecting, and analyzing physical evidence?

Q: It is important to ask about penetration of genitalia?

Q: It is important to ask what was used for penetration?

Q: For example, fingers, a tongue, a penis?

Q: It is important to ask if the anus was penetrated?

Q: It is important to ask about oral contact with genitals?

Q: It is important to ask about oral contact with the anus?

Q: It is important to ask about non-genital acts, for example licking the breasts?

Q: The examiner should ask if licking occurred?

Q: The examiner should ask about kissing?

Q: The examiner should ask about suction injury?

Q: The examiner should ask about strangulation?

Q: The examiner should ask about biting?

Q: The examiner should ask about other sexual acts, including the use of objects?

Point: An examiner must ask whether ejaculation occurred.

Q: It is important to ask whether ejaculation occurred?

Q: It is important to ask about the location of the ejaculation on the body?

Q: It is important to ask if there was ejaculation on other surfaces, such as bedding, clothing, and the floor?

61

FORENSIC STANDARDS

Point: The American Academy of Forensic Sciences has standards.

Q: Now let's talk about the standards set forth by The American Academy of Forensic Sciences, okay?

Q: The American Academy of Forensic Sciences sets forensic standards?

Q: The American Academy of Forensic Sciences is the oldest and largest organization of forensic professionals?

Q: The American Academy of Forensic Sciences sets standards for taking sexual assault photographs?

Q: You are familiar with the proper standards?

Q: It is important to follow the standards?

Q: You were trained on the proper standards?

Q: You have studied the proper standards?

Q: You were even tested on the proper standards?

Q: You passed the test?

Q: You follow the proper standards when you take photographs?

Point: You are required to follow forensic photographic standards.

Q: As a sexual assault examiner, you are required to take photographs of suspected injuries from three different distances?

Q: The first series of photographs you are required to take are the "orientation" photographs showing the body part and the suspected injury?

Q: These are taken at a distance?

Q: The "orientation" photographs show the suspected injury in the total context of the body region involved?

Q: They also show the anatomical orientation of the suspected injury?

Q: The second series of photographs should be taken at a medium distance?

Q: The third series of photographs should be taken at a close distance?

Point: A scale should be used in forensic photography.

Q: When taking photos during the exam, you must make sure you capture the actual size of the injury?

Q: The American Academy of Forensic Sciences requires that you use a scale or a ruler when taking photographs?

Q: Your State protocol also requires that you use a ruler or scale for size reference in the photograph?

Q: You put a scale or ruler in the photo so the size of the injury can be seen?

Q: The scale should be in close proximity to the injury or item being photographed?

Q: The scale should be in the same plane as the injury or item being photographed?

Q: It is required that you take at least two close up photographs of each injury?

Q: It is required that you take one photograph without a scale or ruler?

Q: It is required that you take one photograph with a scale or ruler in the photo?

Q: Taking two photographs in this manner shows the scale was not concealing anything important?

Q: This scale is called a forensic photo scale?

Q: It is also known as a photomacrographic scale or ruler?

Q: These small scales are ideal for close-up photography?

Q: In this case, you did not include a ruler or scale for size reference in the photos?

Point: A color bar should be used in forensic photography.

Q: When taking photos during the exam, you must make sure you capture the accurate color of the injury?

Q: The American Academy of Forensic Sciences requires that you use a color bar when taking photographs?

Q: A color bar is a piece of paper with various colors on it?

Q: Some of the colors are green, red, blue, black, yellow, etc?

Q: The color bar is used to make sure colors are accurately reflected in the photo?

Q: When taking photos, placing a color bar in the photograph ensures accurate color reproduction?

Q: Your State protocol requires that you use a color bar for reference in the photograph?

Q: This is required so the color of the injuries can be verified?

Q: For example, if the color of a suspected injury appears as dark purple, when in fact it is pink, the photo could be misleading?

Q: This is why color accuracy is important when taking sexual assault photographs?

Q: In this case, you did not include a color bar in the photos?

PHOTOGRAPHY BY THE SEXUAL ASSAULT EXAMINER

Point: Photos are crucial to documenting evidence of injuries.

Q: As the examiner, you should take photographs of the patient's anatomy that was involved in the assault?

Q: These photographs are part of the forensic examination process in sexual assault cases?

Q: Such photographs supplement the medical forensic history?

Q: Photographs supplement the evidence documentation?

Q: Photographs supplement the physical findings?

Q: However, photographs cannot substitute for the exam?

Q: Photographs cannot substitute for the report?

Point: Photographs must document physical findings.

Q: Photographs document physical findings?

Q: Photographs document injuries to the patient?

Q: Photographs document injuries to the alleged assailant?

Q: Photographs may be the only way to adequately document findings such as bite marks and bruises?

Q: Photographs are the best way document injuries such as bite marks and bruises?

Q: You are required to photograph every potentially significant injury or finding?

Q: Photographs can be taken by a law enforcement agency?

Q: Photographs can be taken by a forensic medical examiner?

Q: Either way, photographs must be taken?

Q: The photographs should accurately depict the suspected injuries?

Point: Different examiners have different views on sexual assault photographs.

Q: Different examiners have different views on sexual assault photographs?

Q: Some examiners routinely take photographs of detected injuries and uninjured anatomy involved in the assault?

Q: Other examiners limit photographs to detected injuries?

Q: Photographs should not be used to interpret subtle or nonspecific findings that are not noted on exam documentation?

Q: For example, photographs should not be used to interpret subtle or nonspecific findings of "redness" that are not noted on exam documentation?

Q: Photographs cannot reliably diagnose injuries not seen by examiners?

Point: Photos must be clear and accurate.

Q: The examiner is responsible for taking accurate photographs?

Q: The examiner is responsible for taking clear photographs?

Q: The examiner is responsible for taking focused photographs?

Q: With photographs, your goal is to take undistorted photographs?

Q: With photographs, your goal is to take photographs with good perspective?

Q: When taking the photos, you understand that a jury may need to see them one day in court?

Q: The jury may have to make very important decisions based on your photos?

Q: The reason you take photos is to preserve evidence?

Q: Evidence must be preserved in an accurate manner?

Q: Blurry photos are not helpful?

Q: Distorted photos are not helpful?

Q: The examiner is responsible for using adequate lighting?

Point: Shadows in victim photographs can appear as bruises.

Q: The examiner is responsible for taking accurate photographs?

Q: The examiner is responsible for using adequate lighting?

Q: Adequate lighting is important when taking photographs?

Q: A photo with shadows can be misleading?

Q: According to your training, a shadow on a photo of the skin may make the skin look discolored?

Q: According to your training, in a photo where there is a shadow on the skin, the shadow may appear as a bruise?

Q: A shadow may appear as a bruise when there actually is no bruise?

Q: In forensic photography, avoiding shadows on the skin is important?

Point: The use of a flash can change the color of evidence.

Q: The use of a flash can change the color of evidence?

Q: The use of a flash on skin can alter the appearance of the skin in photographs?

Q: The use of a flash on skin can alter the color of the skin in photographs?

Q: Your training teaches that flash photography should not be used in sexual assault examinations?

Q: A high-quality macro lens with good lighting offers the best quality for forensic photography involving sexual assault?

Point: The photos must be focused and undistorted.

Q: When taking forensic photos, you are trained to maintain sharp focus?

Q: When taking forensic photos, you are trained to take clear photos?

Q: You don't want blurry photos?

Q: When taking forensic photos, you are trained to take undistorted photographs?

Q: You are trained to take photographs with good perspective?

Point: The photos must be properly oriented.

Q: You are trained to take at least two shots at three orientations?

Q: You are trained to take medium-range photographs of each separate injury?

Q: This includes suspected cuts, bruises, swelling, lacerations, and abrasions?

Q: You are trained to work from one side to the other and then top to bottom?

Q: You are trained to be consistent with how you take photographs?

Q: You are trained to take "regional" shots to show injuries in the context and orientation of a body region?

Q: These photographs should include easily identifiable anatomical landmarks, such as the armpit or bellybutton?

Q: You are familiar with the American College of Emergency Physicians?

Q: According to the American College of Emergency Physicians' sexual assault protocol, you are required to take at least three photographs of each suspected injury?

Q: According to the American College of Emergency Physicians' sexual assault protocol, when taking a close-up of suspected injuries, you are required to use the scale or a ruler?

Point: A colposcope assists in finding injuries.

Q: The colposcope is an instrument commonly used in sexual assault exams?

Q: The colposcope is like a magnifying glass?

Q: But more complex?

Q: It lets you zoom in and look for injuries to the vagina?

Q: The colposcope has a light?

Q: The colposcope has a magnifying lens?

Q: The colposcope has a camera/recording device?

Q: The colposcope allows the examiner to directly observe and study the tissues?

Point: A colposcope would have seen injuries.

Q: A colposcope has a magnifying lens ranging from 4x to 30x power?

Q: Colposcopes can have camera or video camera attachments?

Q: In addition to a light source, colposcopes have a green filter that enhances the visualization of scars, injuries, and unusual vascular patterns?

Q: A colposcope makes it easier to see injuries to the vagina?

Q: A colposcope makes it easier to photograph injuries?

Q: A colposcope makes it easier to document minor skin and surface trauma?

Q: A colposcope makes it easier to document minor mucosal surface trauma?

Q: A colposcope makes it easier to see abrasions?

Q: A colposcope makes it easier to see lacerations?

Q: A colposcope makes it easier to see hymenal tears?

Q: A colposcope makes it easier to see anal fissures?

Q: In this case, you used a colposcope?

Q: In this case, you did not see any injuries?

CHAPTER 4: COMMONLY USED SEXUAL ASSAULT EXAMINER TERMS

When cross examining a sexual assault examiner, you must know the proper meaning of common medical terminology and be able to explain unknown or confusing terms to the jury in a way they can understand.

The cross examiner must know whether the finding or injury could be attributed to something other than a sexual assault. If so, the jury must be educated on the alternative explanations of certain findings. Otherwise, they may erroneously believe the finding is definitive proof of sexual assault.

GENDER NEUTRAL MEDICAL TERMS

Point: Abrasion defined.

Q: An "abrasion" is an injury or an area of body surface denuded of skin or mucous membrane by some mechanical process?

Point: Anterior defined.

Q: Anterior is the front of or in the forward part of an organ, toward the head of the body?

Q: This is a term used in reference to the ventral or belly surface of the body?

Point: Cephalad defined.

Q: Cephalad is toward the head?

Point: Clock position reference defined.

Q: Clock position reference is a method by which the location of a structure may be designated by using the numerals on the face of a clock?

Q: The 12 o'clock position is always superior or up?

Q: The 6 o'clock position is always inferior or down?

Q: The position of a patient must be indicated when using this designation?

Point: Colposcope defined.

Q: A "colposcope" is an instrument with a light source, a magnifying lens, and sometimes a camera/recording device for direct observation and study of the tissues?

Point: Cuadad defined.

Q: Cuadad is toward the tail?

Point: Cunnilingus defined.

Q: Cunnilingus is the oral stimulation of the female genitalia?

Point: Dorsal defined.

Q: Dorsal pertains to a position toward the back?

Point: Distal defined.

Q: Distal denotes the remoteness from the point of origin or attachment of an organ of part?

Point: Ecchymosis defined.

Q: Ecchymosis is a hemorrhagic area on the skin?

Q: Ecchymosis is caused by extravasation of blood into the skin or a mucous membrane?

Q: Ecchymosis is similar to a bruise?

Point: Elasticity defined.

Q: Elasticity is the state or quality of being distensible?

Q: Capable of being extended or dilated?

Point: Erythema defined.

Q: Erythema is a redness of the skin?

Q: Erythema can also cause redness in a mucous membrane?

Q: It is produced by congestion or dilatation of the capillaries?

Q: It is a non-specific finding?

Q: It can be caused by irritants?

Q: It can be caused by trauma?

Q: It can be caused by inflammation?

Q: It can be caused by infections?

Point: Fellatio defined.

Q: Fellatio is the oral stimulation or manipulation of the penis?

Point: Frog leg position defined.

Q: In the frog leg position, the patient lies in supine (lying on back, face upward) position?

Q: The patient's knees are flexed and hips abducted?

Q: The bottoms of feet touch?

Point: Genitalia (external) defined.

Q: Genitalia (external) are the external sexual organs?

Q: In males, includes the penis and scrotum?

Q: In females, includes the contents of the vulva?

Point: Hyperemia defined.

Q: Hyperemia is an excess of blood in an organ or body part?

Q: It is an engorgement of the blood vessels?

Point: Hyperpigmentation defined.

Q: Hyperpigmentation is the increase in melanin pigment within tissues?

Q: It is a common finding in darker skinned children?

Q: It may be congenital in nature or caused by a past inflammatory response?

Q: Congenital means that it was present from birth?

Point: Inferior defined.

Q: Inferior is below, or directly downward?

Q: This is a term used in reference to the lower surface of an organ or other structure?

Point: Inflammation defined.

Q: Inflammation is a localized protective response of tissues?

Q: It is elicited by injury or destruction of tissues?

Q: When a body part is inflamed, it can show signs of pain?

Q: When a body part is inflamed, it can show signs of redness?

Q: When a body part is inflamed, it can swell?

Q: When a body part is inflamed, it can result in a loss of function?

Point: Intracrural intercourse defined.

Q: Intracrural intercourse is also known as intralabial intercourse?

Q: In lay terms, it is called "dry humping?"

Q: It is the act of rubbing the penis between the labia of the female?

Q: Without entering the vagina?

Point: Knee-chest position method defined.

Q: Knee-chest position method requires the patient to be in a knee-chest position?

Q: While the patient is in this position, the examiner places thumbs beneath the leading edge of the gluteus maximus?

Q: When doing so, the examiner lifts while gently separating labia?

Point: Knee-chest position (prone) defined.

Q: In the knee-chest position (prone), the patient rests on knees with the upper chest on the examination table?

Q: The patient is in a lordotic (sway-backed) posture?

Q: The patient's elbows are flexed with hands placed on either side of the head?

Point: Knee-chest position (supine) defined.

Q: In the knee-chest position (supine) examination position, the patient lies on his/her back?

Q: With the hips flexed upon the abdomen?

Point: Laceration defined.

Q: A laceration is a transection (cut) through the skin, mucous membranes, or deeper structures of the body?

Point: Lateral decubitus (recumbent) examination position defined.

Q: In the lateral decubitus or recumbent examination position, the patient lies on their side?

Q: With the contra lateral thigh and knee drawn up?

Point: Leukocytes defined.

Q: Leukocytes are white blood cells or corpuscles (pus)?

Q: They are part of the inflammatory response to an infection?

Point: Lichenification defined.

Q: Lichenification is the thickening of the skin markings?

Q: It gives the skin a leathery appearance?

Q: It is usually secondary to prolonged irritation secondary to rubbing, scratching, or inflammation?

Point: Lithotomy position (examination position) defined.

Q: In the lithotomy examination position, the patient lies on his/her back?

Q: With his/her hips and knees flexed?

Q: The thighs abducted and externally rotated?

Q: In the prone examination position, the patient lays face downward (on his/her abdomen)?

Point: Median raphe defined.

Q: Now I want to talk about median raphes, do you know what that is?

Q: A median raphe (perineal raphe) is a ridge of tissue?

Q: It is the ridge of tissue that extends from the anus and marks the line of union of the two halves of the perineum?

Q: Some are prominent?

Q: Some are more prominent on men?

Q: Others are barely noticeable?

Q: A normal finding for both men and women may be confused for scars by the untrained observer?

Point: Neovascularization defined.

Q: Neovascularization is the formation of new blood vessels in abnormal tissue or in an abnormal location?

Point: Peri defined.

Q: Peri is a prefix meaning around?

Point: Perineal body defined.

Q: The perineal body is the central tendon of the perineum?

Q: It is located between the vestibule and the anus in the female?

Q: And between the scrotum and anus in the male?

Point: Perineum defined.

Q: The perineum is the area in both males and females between the pubic symphysis and the coccyx?

Q: The perineum is the surface region in both males and females between the pubic symphysis and the coccyx.

Q: The perineum is below the pelvic diaphragm and between the legs?

Q: It is a diamond-shaped area that includes the anus and, in females, the vagina?

Point: Petechiae defined.

Q: Petechiae are small, pinhead-sized hemorrhages?

Q: It is caused by leaking capillaries?

Q: They may be singular or multiple?

Q: They are frequently caused by increased pressure within the blood vessel?

Q: Such as with straining during vomiting or with strangulation?

Q: Petechiae may also be caused by a bleeding disorder?

Q: Petechiae may also be caused by an infection?

Q: Petechiae may also be caused by localized trauma?

Point: Posterior defined.

Q: Posterior is the back of, or in the back part of?

Q: This is a term used in reference to the back or dorsal surface of the body?

Point: Proximal defined.

Q: Proximal is closer to any point of reference?

Point: Scar defined.

Q: A scar is a fibrous tissue?

Q: It is tissue that replaces normal tissue after the healing of a wound?

Q: It may be difficult to prove on clinical grounds?

Q: Such as during visual inspection or palpation alone?

Point: Sodomy defined.

Q: Sodomy is a medical term restricted to anal intercourse?

Point: Straddle injury defined.

Q: A straddle injury is an injury to the perineum?

Q: It is caused when the individual falls on an object while the legs are spread apart?

Point: Superior defined.

Q: Superior is above, or directly upward?

Q: This is a term used in reference to a structure occupying a position near the vertex?

Point: Supine position (examination position) defined.

Q: In the supine examination position, the patient lies (on his/her back) with their face upward?

Point: Synechiae defined.

Q: A synechiae is any adhesion that binds two anatomic structures through the formation of a band of fibrous scar tissue?

Point: Tanner Scales of Secondary Sexual Development defined.

Q: The Tanner Scales of Secondary Sexual Development are a sexual maturity rating scale?

Q: The scale defines the stages of puberty?

Q: In the female, the Tanner Scales use physical evidence such as breast development and pubic hair?

Q: In the male, the Tanner Scales use the testicular/scrotal and penile size plus the location and type of pubic hair?

Q: Stages range from Stage I (prepubertal child) to Stage V (fully mature adult)?

Point: Transection defined.

Q: A transection is a cutting across?

Q: It can also be a division by cutting or tearing transversely?

Point: Urethra defined.

Q: The urethra is a membranous canal?

Q: It conveys urine from the bladder to the exterior of the body?

Point: Urethral dilatation defined.

Q: A urethral dilatation is an enlargement of the urethral meatal aperture?

Q: It is a normal variant when labial traction examination technique is employed?

Point: Urethral meatus defined.

Q: A urethral meatus is an external opening of the canal (urethra)?

Q: It is the opening of the urethra?

Q: It is the point where urine exits the urethra in males and in females?

Q: It is also where semen exits the urethra in males?

Point: Urethritis defined.

Q: Urethritis is the inflammation of the urethra?

Q: Urethritis is a condition in which the urethra, or the tube that carries urine from the bladder to outside the body, becomes inflamed and irritated?

Q: Semen also passes through the male urethra?

Q: Urethritis typically causes pain while urinating and an increased urge to urinate?

Q: The primary cause of urethritis is usually infection by bacteria?

Q: Urethritis affects people of all ages?

Q: Both males and females can develop the condition?

Q: Females have a greater chance of developing the condition than males?

Q: Bacteria found naturally in the genital area may cause urethritis if they enter the urinary tract?

Q: It may be caused by a variety of irritants?

Q: It may be caused by a bubble bath?

Q: It may be caused by other infections?

Point: Vascularity defined.

Q: Vascularity is the dilation of existing superficial blood vessels?

Point: Ventral defined.

Q: Ventral denotes a position more toward the belly surface than some other object of reference?

FEMALE SPECIFIC TERMINOLOGY

Point: Angularity of hymen defined.

Q: The angularity of hymen are relatively sharp angles in the contour of the hymenal inner edge?

Q: When it is located on the posterior hymenal rim and persists during multiple examination techniques, it may be evidence of hymenal trauma?

Point: Annular (circumferential) defined.

Q: The annular (circumferential) is the hymenal membrane that extends completely around the circumference of the vaginal orifice?

Q: It is the most common configuration in the newborn and young infant?

Point: Anterior (superior) hymenal wings (flaps) defined.

Q: The anterior hymenal wings, or flaps, are the bilateral projections of tissue on the anterior (superior) edge of the hymen?

Q: This is a common finding in infants and children less than five years of age?

Q: This is a common finding during the onset of puberty?

Q: They are a normal physiologic tissue response to estrogen?

Point: Asymmetry of fossa navicularis defined.

Q: The asymmetry of fossa navicularis are the posterior commissure attachment of labia minora?

Q: They join the fossa at different levels?

Q: They create an asymmetrical appearance?

Q: They occasionally have a band-like configuration?

Q: It is a relatively common finding of no significance?

Point: Attenuated hymen defined.

Q: An attenuated hymen is the term used to describe areas where the hymen is narrow?

Q: The term is restricted to indicate a documented change in the width of the posterior portion of the hymen following an injury?

Point: Caruncula myrtiformis (hymenales) defined.

Q: Caruncula myrtiformis are small elevations of rounded mounds of hymen?

Q: These encircle the vaginal orifice?

Q: They are found in sexually active and postpartum females?

Point: Cleft/notch defined.

Q: A cleft or notch is an angular or V-shaped indentation on the edge of the hymenal membrane?

Q: It may extend to the muscular attachment of the hymen?

Q: A relatively sharp, V-shaped notch or cleft that persists during multiple examination techniques may be evidence of hymenal trauma?

Point: Cleft (anterior) defined.

Q: An anterior cleft is a shallow indentation of the hymenal membrane?

Q: It does not extend to the attachment of an annular hymen?

Q: Girls with a crescent shaped hymen appear to have an absence of the membrane between the 11 and 1 o'clock positions?

Q: In this situation, the term anterior sparing is preferable?

Q: Newborns frequently have a cleft or notch in the midline of the hymen superiorly?

Point: Cleft (lateral) defined.

Q: A lateral cleft is an indentation along the lateral margins of the hymen?

Q: It is usually found at the 2 to 4 and 8 to 10 o'clock positions with the child supine?

Q: It must be interpreted with caution?

Q: Particularly if there are bilateral, smooth edged, or symmetrical clefts?

Q: Bilateral, smooth edged, or symmetrical clefts may occur naturally?

Q: The lateral cleft may be found in sexually active females?

Point: Cleft (posterior) defined.

Q: A posterior cleft is an indentation in the posterior edge of the hymen?

Q: It is usually found at the 4 to 8 o'clock positions with the child supine?

Q: Clefts in the posterior rim that persist during multiple examination techniques are usually evidence of hymenal trauma?

Point: Clitoris defined.

Q: The clitoris is a small, cylindric, erectile body?

Q: It is situated at the anterior (superior) portion of the vulva?

Q: It is covered by a sheath of skin called the clitoral hood?

Q: It is homologous with the penis in the male?

Point: Clitoral hood defined.

Q: The clitoral hood is the skin covering the clitoris?

Q: It is homologous with the prepuce (foreskin) in the male?

Q: It may become inflamed from contact with a variety of irritants, or from trauma?

Point: Clue cells defined.

Q: Clue cells are vaginal epithelial cells with clusters of bacteria adhering to the surface?

Q: Clue cells are common in sexually active females?

Point: Complete hymenal defined.

Q: A complete hymenal is a tear or laceration through the entire width of the hymenal membrane?

Q: It extends to the hymenal membrane's attachments to the vaginal wall?

Point: Concavity defined.

Q: Concavity or depression is a curved or hollowed U-shaped depression on the edge of the hymenal membrane?

Point: Crescentic hymen defined.

Q: A crescentic hymen is a hymen with anterior attachments?

Q: The attachments are at approximately the 11 o'clock and the 1 o'clock positions?

Q: There is no hymenal tissue visible between the two attachments?

Q: This is the most common hymenal configuration in the school aged and prepubescent child?

Point: Cribriform hymen defined.

Q: A cribriform hymen is a hymen with multiple openings?

Q: It is a congenital variant?

Q: Congenital means that it was present from birth?

Point: Cyst (hymenal) defined.

Q: A hymenal cyst is a fluid-filled sac of tissue?

Q: It is confined within the hymenal tissue?

Q: It is considered to be a normal variant?

Point: Denticular hymen (fimbriated) defined.

Q: A denticular hymen is a hymen with multiple projections or indentations along the edge?

Q: It creates a ruffled appearance?

Q: It is a congenital variant?

Q: Congenital means that it was present from birth?

Point: Erythema of the hymen defined.

Q: An erythema of the hymen is a redness of the hymenal membrane?

Q: It is produced by congestion or engorgement of the capillaries?

Q: It is a non-specific finding?

Q: It may result from a variety of irritants as well as direct trauma?

Point: Estrogenization defined

Q: Estrogenization is the effect or influence by the female sex hormone estrogen?

Q: Estrogenization causes changes to the genitalia?

Point: External hymenal ridge defined.

Q: An external hymenal ridge is a midline, longitudinal ridge of tissue?

Q: It is on the external surface of the hymen?

Q: It can be either anterior or posterior?

Q: It usually extends to the edge of the membrane?

Q: It is a congenital variant most commonly found during the newborn period or infancy?

Q: Congenital means that it was present from birth?

Point: Fimbriated hymen (denticular) defined.

Q: A fimbriated hymen is a hymen with multiple projections or indentations along the edge?

Q: It creates a ruffled appearance?

Q: It is a congenital variant?

Q: Congenital means that it was present from birth?

Point: Follicles defined.

Q: Follicles are small, clear or yellow-colored papules on the hymen and/or surrounding tissues?

Q: They are usually 1-2 millimeters each?

Q: They appear to contain lymph-like material?

Point: Fordyce's Granule defined.

Q: Fordyce's Granule is an ectopic sebaceous gland?

Q: Found on the labia?

Q: And it presents as a yellowish-white milia or papule?

Point: Fossa navicularis defined.

Q: The fossa navicularis is the concavity of the lower part of the vestibule?

Q: It is situated posterior (inferior) to the vaginal orifice?

Q: It extends to the posterior fourchette (posterior commissure)?

Q: It may be injured as a result of a straddle injury?

Q: It may also be injured in a sexual assault?

Q: It can also be injured during consensual sexual intercourse?

Point: Friability defined.

Q: Friability is a superficial breakdown of the skin of the posterior commissure?

Q: It happens when gentle traction is applied?

Q: It can cause slight bleeding?

Q: It is considered a non-specific finding?

Point: Friability of the posterior fourchette defined.

Q: Friability of the posterior fourchette is a superficial breakdown of the skin in the posterior fourchette?

Q: When gentle traction is applied, causing slight bleeding?

Point: Hymen defined.

Q: The hymen is a membrane that covers the external vaginal orifice?

Q: The hymenal membranes partially cover the external vaginal orifice?

Q: Rarely does the membrane completely cover the external vaginal orifice?

Q: The hymen is located at the junction of the vestibular floor and the vaginal canal?

Q: The external surface is lined with highly differentiated squamous epithelium, with loose cornification?

Q: The internal surface is lined with vaginal epithelium?

Q: It's origin is the external vaginal plate of the urogenital sinus?

Q: There is wide variation in types of hymens?

Q: There is the annular hymen?

Q: There is the crescentic hymen?

Q: There is the fimbriated (denticular) hymen?

Q: There is the septate hymen?

Q: There is the cribriform hymen?

Q: There is the imperforate?

Q: All hymens are different?

Q: They vary widely in characteristics?

Q: Some are redundant and thick?

Q: Some are smooth and thin?

Q: The characteristics vary depending upon age and stage of secondary sexual development?

Q: All females with a normal Mullerian system have a hymen?

Q: All females with normal external genitalia have a hymen?

Point: Hymenal inflammation defined.

Q: Hymenal inflammation is a localized protective response?

Q: It is elicited by injury or destruction of tissues?

Q: It is a non-specific finding?

Q: It can result from a variety of causes including trauma?

Point: Hymenal Notch/cleft defined.

Q: A hymenal notch or cleft is an angular or V-shaped indentation?

86

Q: It is on the edge of the hymenal membrane?

Q: It may extend to the muscular attachment of the hymen?

Q: It is a relatively sharp, V-shaped notch or cleft?

Q: It may be evidence of hymenal trauma?

Point: Hymenal orifice defined.

Q: A hymenal orifice is the opening in the hymenal membrane?

Q: It is the entrance or outlet of the vagina?

Point: Hymenal orifice's diameter defined.

Q: The hymenal orifice's diameter is the distance from one edge of the hymen to the opposite edge of the hymenal orifice?

Q: The most common measurement used is the horizontal/lateral diameter?

Q: The size varies with the age of the child, the examination technique, and other factors, such as the state of relaxation?

Q: The size of the hymenal orifice should be used with caution in determining if prior sexual abuse has occurred?

Q: There are multiple reasons why a hymenal orifice may appear larger than normal?

Point: Hymenales defined.

Q: Hymenales are small elevations of rounded mounds of hymen?

Q: These encircle the vaginal orifice?

Q: They are found in sexually active and postpartum females?

Point: Imperforate defined.

Q: An imperforate is a hymenal membrane with no opening?

Q: It is an uncommon congenital variant?

Q: Congenital means that it was present from birth?

Point: Intact hymen defined.

Q: An intact hymen is an antiquated term implying a non-injured hymenal membrane?

Point: Intravaginal columns defined.

Q: Intravaginal columns are raised, sagittally oriented columns?

Q: They are most prominent on the anterior wall, with less prominence on the posterior wall?

Point: Intravaginal longitudinal ridges defined.

Q: Intravaginal longitudinal ridges are narrow, mucosa-covered ridges of tissue on the vaginal wall?

Q: They may be attached to the inner surface of the hymen?

Q: They may be located in all four quadrants, and are usually multiple in number?

Q: This is a normal finding?

Point: Irregular hymenal edge defined

Q: An irregular hymenal edge is a disruption in the smooth contour of the hymen?

Point: Key-hole configuration defined.

Q: A key-hole configuration is a key-hole appearance of the hymenal orifice?

Q: It is created when the posterior-lateral portions of the hymenal membrane project into the orifice?

Q: It creates a concavity inferiorly?

Point: Labial adhesion defined.

Q: A labial adhesion is the result of adherence or fusion?

Q: This adherence occurs in the adjacent, outer-most mucosal surfaces of the posterior portion vestibular walls?

Q: This may occur at any point along the length of the vestibule?

Q: Most commonly it occurs posteriorly (inferiorly)?

Q: It is a common finding in infants and young children?

Q: It usually appears for the first time after 6 to 7 years of age?

Q: It may be related to chronic irritation?

Point: Labia majora (outer lips) defined.

Q: The labia majora is known as the outer lips?

Q: The labia majora are rounded folds of skin?

Q: They form the lateral boundaries of the vulva?

Point: Labia minora (inner lips) defined.

Q: The labia minora are known as the inner lips?

Q: The labia minora are the two inner folds (lips) of tissue, between the labia majora and the hymenal ring, and within the vulva?

Q: The labia minora is contained within the vulva?

Point: Labial separation method defined.

Q: While using the labial separation method, the labia majora are gently separated?

Q: This is done in a lateral and downward direction?

Q: Doing so exposes the vestibule?

Point: Labial traction method defined.

Q: In the labial traction method, the labia majora are grasped between the thumbs and index fingers and gently pulled toward the examiner?

Q: The patient is usually in the supine position?

Point: Laceration of the hymen defined.

Q: A laceration of the hymen is an injury or tear of the hymenal membrane?

Q: That is usually associated with blunt force penetration?

Point: Leukorrhea defined.

Q: Leukorrhea is a whitish, viscid (glutinous) discharge?

Q: It is discharged through the vagina and uterine cavity?

Q: It is a normal finding in adolescent and adult females?

Point: Linea vestibularis defined.

Q: The linea vestibularis is a vertical, pale/vascular appearing line?

Q: It is also known as the midline sparing?

Q: The line goes across the posterior fourchette and/or fossa navicularis?

Q: It may be accentuated by putting lateral traction on the labia majora?

Q: It is a common finding in girls of all ages?

Q: It is also a common finding in newborns and adolescents?

Point: Marital introitus defined.

Q: Marital introitus is an enlarged hymenal orifice?

Point: Median perineal raphe defined.

Q: The median perineal raphe is a ridge or furrow?

Q: It marks the line of union of the two halves of the perineum?

Point: Midline commissure defined.

Q: A midline commissure is the site of union of the anterior or posterior commissure of the labia minora?

Point: Mons pubis defined.

Q: The mons pubis is the rounded fleshy prominence found in the vagina?

Q: It is created by the underlying fat pad, which lies over the pubic bone?

Point: Mound defined.

Q: A mound or bump is a solid, localized, rounded and thickened area of tissue on the edge of the hymen?

Q: It may be created by the hymenal attachment of a longitudinal intravaginal ridge?

Point: Narrow hymenal membrane defined.

Q: Narrow hymenal membrane is the term used to describe the width of the hymenal membrane?

Q: The narrow hymenal membrane is also known as rim attenuated?

Q: It is viewed in the coronal plane, i.e. from the edge of the hymen to the muscular portion of the vaginal introitus (opening)?

Q: An abnormally narrow hymenal membrane may be evidence of prior trauma?

Point: Partial hymenal defined.

Q: A partial hymenal is a tear or laceration through a portion of the hymenal membrane?

Q: It does not extend to the hymenal membrane's attachment to the vaginal wall?

Point: Pelvic inflammatory disease defined.

Q: Pelvic inflammatory disease is an infection?

Q: It is an infection of the uterus, fallopian tubes and/or ovaries?

Point: Perihymenal defined.

Q: The phrase perihymenal pertains to tissues surrounding the hymen?

Point: Perihymenal bands defined.

Q: Perihymenal bands are small bands of tissue?

Q: They are lateral to the hymen?

Q: They form a connection between the perihymenal structures and the wall of the vestibule?

Q: They are a less frequently observed finding than periurethral bands in prepubescent girls?

Q: They are accentuated when the labial traction examination method is used?

Q: They are usually a congenital variation?

Q: Congenital means that it was present from birth?

Q: They are rarely caused by trauma?

Point: Perineal groove defined.

Q: The perineal groove is a developmental anomaly?

Q: It is also called "failure of fusion?"

Q: It is a midline defect in the median raphe?

Q: It happens when the skin and/or mucosal surfaces fail to fuse?

Q: It may involve any part of the median raphe, from the fossa to the anus?

Point: Periurethral defined.

Q: Periurethral pertains to tissue surrounding the urethral meatus?

Point: Periurethral bands defined.

Q: Periurethral bands are small bands?

Q: They are lateral to the urethra?

Q: They connect the periurethral tissues to the wall of the vestibule?

Q: These bands are usually symmetrical?

Q: They frequently create a semilunar shaped space between the bands on either side of the urethral meatus?

Q: They are also called urethral support ligaments?

Q: They are found in the majority of females?

Q: They are accentuated when the labial traction examination technique is used?

Point: Posterior commissure defined.

Q: A posterior commissure is the union of the two labia posteriorly (toward the anus)?

Q: This area is referred to as a posterior commissure in the prepubescent child?

Q: In children, the labia minora are not completely developed?

Q: In children, the labia minora do not connect inferiorly until puberty?

Q: In the postpubescent female, it is referred to as the posterior fourchette?

Q: It may be injured as the result of a straddle injury?

Q: It may be injured by nonconsensual sexual intercourse?

Q: It may be injured during consensual sexual intercourse?

Point: Posterior fornix defined.

Q: The posterior fornix is a cavity within the vagina and located posteriorly (inferior) to the cervix?

Point: Posterior fourchette defined.

Q: The posterior fourchette is a fork-shaped fold of skin at the bottom of the entrance to the vagina.

Q: It is at the 6 o'clock position?

Q: Fourchette means fork?

Q: It is a junction of two sides of the labia minora?

Q: Vulvar pain may be due to recurrent fissuring or splitting of the posterior fourchette?

Q: Pain from fissuring is often described as being 'like a paper-cut' or 'knife-like'?

Q: This area is referred to as a posterior commissure in the prepubescent child?

Q: In children, the labia minora are not completely developed and do not connect inferiorly until puberty?

Q: In the postpubescent female, it is referred to as the posterior fourchette?

Point: Redundant hymen defined.

Q: A redundant hymen has abundant hymenal tissue?

Q: It tends to fold back upon itself or protrude?

Q: It is a common finding in females whose hymenal membranes are under the influence of estrogen (both infants and adolescents)?

Point: Rolled edges defined.

Q: Rolled edges refer to the edge or border of the hymen?

Q: They tend to roll inward or outward upon itself?

Q: They may unfold with the knee-chest position?

Q: They may unfold with the application of water?

Q: They may unfold through manipulation with a moistened Q-tip?

Q: They may unfold with other techniques?

Q: Rolled edges are a normal variant most commonly noted in prepubescent children?

Point: Rounded edges defined.

Q: Rounded edges are hymenal edges?

Q: They appear thick and rounded?

Q: They do not thin out with the different examination techniques?

Q: They do not thin out with the application of water, or other maneuvers used to unroll an elastic, redundant hymen?

Q: They may be the result of hormonal influence?

Q: They may be the result of poor relaxation?

Q: They may be the result of an inflammatory reaction?

Q: They may be the result of the attachment of an underlying intravaginal longitudinal ridge?

Q: They may be the result of past injury?

Point: Rugae (vaginal) defined.

Q: The vaginal rugae are folds of epithelium (rugae)?

Q: They run circumferentially from the vaginal columns?

Q: This is a normal finding?

Point: Scalloped edges defined.

Q: Scalloped edges are a series of rounded projections?

Q: They are along the edge of the hymen?

Q: They are a common finding in early adolescence?

Point: Septal remnant (hymen subseptus) defined.

Q: A septal remnant is a small appendage attached to the edge of the hymen?

Q: It is commonly located in the midline on the posterior rim?

Q: It is frequently associated with a concomitant thickened ridge on the hymen, which extends from the appendage to the muscular attachment of the vaginal introitus?

Q: It may be associated with similar appendage on the opposite side of the hymenal orifice?

Q: It is considered to be a normal variant?

Point: Septated hymen defined.

Q: A septated hymen is a hymen with band(s) of tissue?

Q: It bisects the orifice creating two or more openings?

Q: It is a congenital variant?

Q: Congenital means that it was present from birth?

Point: Tag (hymenal) defined.

Q: A tag is an elongated projection of tissue?

Q: A hymenal tag arises from any location on the hymenal rim?

Q: It is commonly found in the midline?

Q: It may be an extension of a posterior vaginal ridge?

Q: It is usually a congenital variant?

Q: Congenital means that it was present from birth?

Q: It is rarely caused by trauma?

Point: Thickened edge defined.

Q: The thickened edge is a term used to describe the relative amount of tissue between the internal and external surfaces of the hymenal membrane?

Q: It may be the result of hormonal influence?

Q: It may be the result of poor relaxation?

Q: It may be the result of the attachment of an underlying intravaginal longitudinal ridge?

Q: It may be the result of a past injury?

Point: Transection of the hymen (complete) defined.

Q: A complete transection of the hymen is a tear or laceration?

Q: It transects the entire width of the hymenal membrane?

Q: It extends to or through its attachment to the vaginal wall?

Point: Transection of the hymen (partial) defined.

Q: A partial transection of the hymen is a tear or laceration?

Q: It goes through a portion of the hymenal membrane?

Q: It does not extend to its attachment to the vaginal wall?

Point: Urethral prolapse defined.

Q: A urethral prolapse is a protrusion of the distal urethra through the external meatus?

Q: It is a rarely diagnosed condition?

Q: It occurs most commonly in prepubescent black females, and postmenopausal white women?

Q: It may present as bleeding from the female genitalia?

Q: It is most commonly seen in African American children?

Q: Its relationship to sexual abuse has not yet been determined?

Point: Vagina defined.

Q: The vagina is the genital canal in the female?

Q: It extends from the uterine cervix to the inner aspect of the hymen?

Point: Vaginal introitus defined.

Q: The vaginal introitus is the pubovaginalis muscle?

Q: It forms the entrance to the vagina?

Q: It is frequently used synonymously with hymenal orifice?

Point: Vaginitis defined.

Q: Vaginitis is the inflammation of the vagina?

Q: It may be marked by a purulent discharge and discomfort?

Q: It may be caused by a variety of conditions?

Q: It may be caused by bacterial vaginosis?

Q: It may be caused by sexually transmitted diseases?

Q: It may be caused by foreign bodies?

Point: Vestibule (vaginal) defined.

Q: The vaginal vestibule is the union of the two labia minora anteriorly (toward the clitoris)?

Q: It may be torn as a result of a straddle injury?

Q: It may be torn by forceful separation of the labia minora?

Point: Vulva defined.

Q: The vulva is the external genitalia of the female?

Q: It includes the mons pubis?

Q: It includes the clitoris?

Q: It includes the labia majora?

Q: It includes the labia minora?

Q: It includes the vaginal vestibule?

Q: It includes the urethral orifice?

Q: It includes the vaginal orifice?

Q: It includes the hymen?

Q: It includes the posterior fourchette?

Point: Vulvar coitus defined.

Q: Vulvar coitus involves rubbing of the penis between the labia of the female without entering the vagina?

Point: Vulvitis defined.

Q: Vulvitis is the inflammation of the labia and vestibule?

Q: It may be caused by a variety of irritants?

Q: It may be caused by improper wiping techniques?

Q: It may be caused by poor hygiene?

Q: It may be caused by bubble bath?

Q: It may be caused by shampoo?

Q: It may be caused by infectious agents?

MALE SPECIFIC TERMINOLOGY

Point: Balanitis defined.

Q: Balanitis is the inflammation of the glans penis?

Q: It is usually associated with phimosis?

Q: It is usually a non-specific finding?

Point: Corona of glans penis defined.

Q: The corona of glans penis is the rounded proximal border of the glans penis?

Q: It is separated from the corpora cavernosa penis by the neck of the glans?

Point: Frenulum defined.

Q: The frenulum is a small fold of mucus membrane?

Q: It attaches the prepuce to the ventral surface of the penis?

Point: Glans penis defined.

Q: The glans penis is the cap-shaped expansion of the corpus spongiosum at the end (head) of the penis?

Q: It is also called the balanus?

Q: It is covered by a mucus membrane?

Q: It is sheathed by the foreskin in the uncircumcised male?

Point: Median (perineal) raphe defined.

Q: Median raphe is a ridge or furrow?

Q: A median raphe is also known as a perineal raphe?

Q: It marks the line of union of the two halves of the perineum?

Point: Paraphimosis defined.

Q: Paraphimosis is the retraction of the phimotic foreskin?

Q: It causes a painful swelling of the glans?

Q: If severe, it may cause dry gangrene unless corrected?

Point: Penis defined.

Q: The penis is the male sex organ?

Q: It is composed of erectile tissue?

Q: The urethra passes through the penis?

Q: The penis is homologous with the clitoris in the female?

Q: The penis is rarely injured as the result of sexually motivated abuse?

Point: Perineal (median) raphe defined.

Q: Perineal raphe is a ridge or furrow?

Q: It marks the line of union of the two halves of the perineum?

Point: Phimosis defined.

Q: Phimosis is the constriction of the preputial orifice?

Q: Which limits the retraction of the foreskin back over the glans?

Point: Posthitis defined.

Q: Posthitis is inflammation of the foreskin?

Point: Prepuce (foreskin) defined.

Q: The prepuce is the foreskin on the penis?

Q: It is a covering fold of skin over the glans of the penis?

Point: Prostate defined.

Q: The prostate is a male gland?

Q: It contributes to the seminal fluid?

Q: It accounts for the liquefaction of the coagulated semen?

Point: Scrotum defined.

Q: The scrotum is the pouch that contains the testicles?

Q: It also contains accessory organs?

Point: Testes defined.

Q: The testes are the male sex organs (gonads)?

Q: They are also known as the gonads?

Q: The testes produce spermatozoa and testosterone?

Point: Urethra defined.

Q: The urethra is the membranous canal which conveys urine from the bladder to the exterior of the body?

Point: Urethral meatus (orifice) defined.

Q: The urethral meatus is the external opening of the canal leading from the bladder?

Point: Urethritis defined.

Q: Urethritis is the inflammation of the urethra?

Q: Urethritis is a condition in which the urethra, or the tube that carries urine from the bladder to outside the body, becomes inflamed and irritated?

Q: Semen also passes through the male urethra?

Q: Urethritis typically causes pain while urinating and an increased urge to urinate?

Q: The primary cause of urethritis is usually infection by bacteria?

Q: Urethritis affects people of all ages?

Q: Both males and females can develop the condition?

Q: Females have a greater chance of developing the condition than males?

Q: Bacteria found naturally in the genital area may cause urethritis if they enter the urinary tract?

Q: It may be caused by a variety of irritants?

Q: It may be caused by a bubble bath?

Q: It may be caused by other infections?

Point: Vas deferens defined.

Q: The vas deferens is the excretory duct of the testicle?

Q: The vas deferens passes from the testis to the ejaculatory duct?

TERMS RELATING TO THE ANUS

Point: Anal dilation (dilatation) defined.

Q: Anal dilation is when the anus opens?

Q: It is secondary to relaxation of the external (and possibly the internal) anal sphincter muscles?

Q: It occurs with minimal traction on the buttocks?

Q: This is a finding that must be interpreted with caution?

Q: Anal dilatations have been observed in abused children?

Q: Anal dilatations have been observed in non-abused children?

Q: It is associated with a variety of causes?

Q: It is associated with sedation?

Q: It is associated with anesthesia?

Q: It is associated with trauma?

Q: Anal dilation can be caused by consensual anal sex?

Q: Anal dilation can be caused by non-consensual anal sex?

Q: Anal dilation can be caused by sex toys?

Q: Anal dilation can be caused by other objects inserted into the anus?

Q: It is a common post mortem finding?

Point: Anal fissure defined.

Q: An anal fissure is a superficial break or split in the perianal skin, which radiates out from the anal orifice?

Q: It is associated with a variety of causes?

Q: It can be caused by the passage of hard stools?

Q: It can be caused by trauma?

Q: It can be caused by constipation?

Q: It can be caused by diseases such as Crohn's Disease?

Q: It can be caused by consensual anal sex?

Q: It can be caused by non-consensual anal sex?

Q: It can be caused by sex toys?

Q: It can be caused by other objects inserted into the anus?

Point: Anal laxity defined.

Q: Anal laxity is the decrease in muscle tone of the anal sphincters?

Q: It results in dilation of the anus?

Q: It may occur immediately following an acute or forced sodomy?

Q: It can be caused by a damaged sphincter?

Q: It can be caused by consensual anal sex?

Q: It can be caused by non-consensual anal sex?

Q: It can be caused by sex toys?

Q: It can be caused by other objects inserted into the anus?

Point: Anal skin tag defined.

Q: An anal skin tag is a protrusion of anal verge tissue?

Q: An anal skin tag interrupts the symmetry of the perianal skin folds?

Q: It is a projection of tissue on the perianal skin?

Q: When located outside the midline, causes other than a congenital variation should be considered?

Q: Congenital means that it was present from birth?

Q: It could be caused by Crohn's disease?

Q: It could be caused by trauma?

Q: It can be caused by consensual anal sex?

Q: It can be caused by non-consensual anal sex?

Q: It can be caused by sex toys?

Q: It can be caused by other objects inserted into the anus?

Point: Anal spasm defined.

Q: An anal spasm is an involuntary contraction?

Q: It occurs in the anal sphincter muscles?

Q: It may be accompanied by pain?

Q: It may cause interference with function?

Q: It may be found immediately after anal sex?

Q: It can be caused by consensual anal sex?

Q: It can be caused by non-consensual anal sex?

Q: It can be caused by sex toys?

Q: It can be caused by other objects inserted into the anus?

Point: Anal verge defined.

Q: The anal verge is the tissue overlying the subcutaneous external anal sphincter?

Q: It is at the most distal portion of the anal canal?

Q: It extends exteriorly to the margin of the anal skin?

Point: Anal wink defined.

Q: An anal wink is the reflex of the anal sphincter muscle?

Q: It is a contraction as a result of stroking the perianal skin?

Q: It is used to determine sensory nerve function?

Q: Its relationship to sexual abuse is unknown?

Point: Anus defined.

Q: The anus is the anal orifice?

Q: The anus is the lower opening of the digestive tract?

Q: The anus is at the center of the fold between the buttocks?

Point: Dentate line (pectinate line) defined.

Q: The dentate line is also called the pectinate line?

Q: The dentate line is the saw-toothed line between the lower portion of the anal valves and the pectin?

Q: It is a smooth zone of simple stratified epithelium?

Q: It extends to the anal verge?

Q: The dentate line only appears when the external and internal anal sphincters relax and the anus dilates?

Q: A dentate line is a common finding in an autopsy?

Point: Diastasis ani (smooth area) defined.

Q: Diastasis ani is a smooth, often V or wedge-shaped area?

Q: It is located at either the 6 or 12 o'clock positions in the perianal region?

Q: Its appearance is due to the absence of the underlying corrugator external anal sphincter muscle?

Q: It is a result of the loss of the usual anal skin folds in the area?

Q: It is a congenital variant?

Q: Congenital means that it was present from birth?

Point: Ecchymosis of the perianal tissues defined.

Q: Ecchymosis of the perianal tissues is a hemorrhagic area (bruise)?

Q: It occurs on the skin or mucous membrane of the perianal tissues?

Q: It is due to extravasation of blood?

Q: It is most commonly caused by external trauma?

Q: It can be caused by sexual activity?

Q: It can be caused by consensual sexual activity?

Q: It can be caused by non-consensual sexual activity?

Q: It can be caused by other things as well?

Q: It may be confused with venous congestion and postmortem lividity?

Point: Edema (swelling) defined.

Q: Edema is the presence of abnormal amounts of fluid in the intercellular space?

Q: Edema is also known as swelling?

Q: It can be caused by consensual sexual activity?

Q: It can be caused by non-consensual sexual activity?

Q: If secondary to trauma, it will usually be accompanied by erythema, pain, and swelling of perianal skin folds?

Point: Erythema (perianal) defined.

Q: Erythema (perianal) is a redness of the skin or mucous membranes?

Q: It is due to congestion of the capillaries?

Q: It is a non-specific finding?

Q: It may result from a variety of causes?

Q: It may result from improper hygiene?

Q: It may result from infection?

Q: It may result from trauma?

Q: It can be caused by consensual anal sex?

Q: It can be caused by non-consensual anal sex?

Q: It can be caused by use of sex toys?

Q: It can be caused by other objects inserted into the anus?

Point: Fistula-in-ano defined.

Q: Fistula-in-ano results from developmental abnormalities of the mucosal glands at the base of the anal crypts?

Q: It usually manifests as a draining pustule in the first year of life?

Q: More common in males?

Q: It is four times more likely in boys than in girls?

Point: Flattened anal skin folds defined.

Q: Flattened anal skin folds are a reduction or absence of the perianal folds or wrinkles?

Q: They are common when the external anal sphincter is partially or completely relaxed?

Q: The relationship to sexual abuse is unknown?

Q: It is a common finding in sedated, relaxed children, and at autopsy?

Point: Funnel appearance defined.

Q: A funnel appearance is a decrease in the fatty (subcutaneous) tissue surrounding the anus?

Q: This leads to a concave appearance?

Q: Its relationship to sexual abuse is unknown?

Point: Hemorrhoid defined.

Q: A hemorrhoid is when a varicose vein dilates, or enlarges?

Q: This occurs in the superior or inferior hemorrhoidal plexus?

Q: It is caused by a persistent increase in venous pressure?

Point: Hyperpigmentation defined.

Q: Hyperpigmentation is the increase in melanin pigment?

Q: This occurs within the anal tissues?

Q: This is a common congenital finding in darker skinned children?

Q: Congenital means that it was present from birth?

Q: It may be associated with post-inflammatory changes?

Point: Intermittent anal dilation defined.

Q: Intermittent anal dilation is when the anus dilates sporadically?

Q: This occurs during a medical examination?

Q: It is common in the prone knee-chest position?

Q: It is a common finding in children of all ages?

Point: Lacerations (perianal) defined.

Q: A perianal laceration is a tear?

Q: It is a tear in the tissues immediately surrounding the anus?

Q: A perianal laceration may result from a variety of causes?

Q: A perianal laceration may result from the passage of hard stools?

Q: A perianal laceration may result from the insertion of foreign objects?

Q: A perianal laceration may result from the insertion of a penis?

Q: A perianal laceration may result from the insertion of a dildo?

Q: Failure of fusion of the median raphe may simulate a laceration?

Q: It can be caused by consensual anal sex?

Q: It can be caused by non-consensual anal sex?

Q: It can be caused by sex toys?

Q: It can be caused by other objects inserted into the anus?

Point: Pectinate line (dentate line) defined.

Q: The pectinate line is also called the dentate line?

Q: The pectinate line is the saw-toothed line between the lower portion of the anal valves and the pectin?

Q: It is a smooth zone of simple stratified epithelium?

Q: Which extends to the anal verge?

Q: The pectinate line only appears when the external and internal anal sphincters relax and the anus dilates?

Q: A pectinate line is a common finding at autopsy?

Point: Perianal skin folds defined.

Q: Perianal skin folds are wrinkles or folds?

Q: They are wrinkles or folds of perianal or anal skin?

Q: They radiate from the anus?

Q: They are common in all humans?

Q: They are created by the contraction of the external anal sphincter?

Point: Perianal venous congestion defined.

Q: A perianal venous congestion is the collection of venous blood?

Q: It is the collection of venous blood in the venous plexus of the perianal tissues?

Q: It creates a flat, purple discoloration?

Q: It may be localized or diffuse?

Q: It is a common finding in children?

Q: It can be caused when the thighs are flexed upon the hips for an extended period of time?

Point: Perianal venous engorgement (pooling) defined.

Q: Perianal venous engorgement (pooling) is the pooling of venous blood in the perianal tissues?

Q: This engorgement creates a bluish-purple bulging of the tissues?

Q: It may be localized or diffuse?

Q: Its significance to sexual assault is currently unknown?

Point: Rectum defined.

Q: The rectum is the distal portion of the large intestine?

Q: The rectum begins anterior to the third sacral vertebra?

Q: It is a continuation of the sigmoid?

Q: It ends at the anal canal?

Point: Reflex anal dilatation defined.

Q: A reflex anal dilatation is an involuntary anal dilation?

Q: A reflex anal dilatation occurs upon stroking the buttocks?

Q: A reflex anal dilatation was once considered evidence of prior sexual abuse?

Q: According to modern medicine, its relationship to sexual abuse is unclear?

Q: A reflex anal dilatation is sometimes called an anal wink?

Point: Scars of perianal tissues defined.

Q: Scars of perianal tissues are scar formations?

Q: They are scars in the tissues immediately surrounding the anus?

Q: Perianal scars are usually a result of prior trauma?

Q: The scars can be caused by consensual anal sex?

Q: The scars can be caused by non-consensual anal sex?

Q: The scars can be caused by sex toys?

Q: The scars can be caused by other objects inserted into the anus?

Q: Perianal scars are a common finding?

Q: Injured anal tissues heal rapidly?

Q: When anal injuries heal, they leave little evidence of prior trauma?

Q: Diastasis ani, a congenital variation, may be confused with scar formation?

Q: Congenital means that it was present from birth?

Point: Shallow anal canal defined.

Q: A shallow anal canal is a result of the relaxation of the anal sphincter muscles?

Q: A shallow anal canal can cause a flattening of the anal verge?

Q: This may lead to exposure of the pectinate line and the anal canal?

Q: This is a common finding during anesthesia?

Q: This is a common finding following sedation and at autopsy?

Q: Its relationship to sexual abuse is unknown?

CHAPTER 5: CROSS EXAMINING WITNESSES REGARDING FORENSIC EVIDENCE

FORENSIC EXPERTS AND CRIME SCENE INVESTIGATORS

In sexual assault cases involving physical, forensic, or scientific evidence, forensic experts and crime scene investigators often testify for the prosecution. Their testimony can make or break a case. These witnesses are usually difficult to control and will try to embarrass the cross examiner, especially if the cross examiner is unprepared. Therefore, the cross examiner must know the proper procedures for collecting, preserving, and testing forensic evidence. Additionally, the cross examiner must ask simple questions in order to control the witness and convey reasonable doubt to the jury. The questions in this chapter are based on modern forensic principles found in learned treatises, scientific journals, and law enforcement manuals.

BASICS OF FORENSIC EVIDENCE COLLECTION AND HANDLING

Point: Forensic evidence must be handled carefully.

Q: Witnesses to a crime might recall the events of the crime differently from one another?

Q: Physical evidence can help sort out conflicts in different witness statements?

Q: For example, a person's fingerprint in a room may disprove a person's statement that they were never in that room?

Q: The collecting of evidence is critical to the integrity of an investigation?

Q: The processing of evidence is critical to the integrity of an investigation?

Q: In a sexual assault case, there can be several kinds of physical evidence?

Q: Some evidence is very small?

Q: Some evidence can be difficult to see with the naked eye?

Q: Some evidence can be impossible to see with the naked eye?

Q: Evidence can include body hairs?

Q: It can include body fluids?

Q: It can include fibers?

Q: It can include skins cells?

Q: This type of evidence is often small?

Q: This type of evidence is often sensitive to environmental conditions?

Q: This type of evidence is sensitive to humidity?

Q: This type of evidence is sensitive to heat?

Q: Investigators must be careful not to overlook this type of evidence?

Q: With new forensic technology, crime scene investigation has become more complex than it was decades ago?

Q: Evidence has to be handled carefully to make sure it is not damaged or degraded?

Point: Numerous people handled the evidence.

Q: In this case, many people were involved in the collection and processing of the evidence?

Q: There was the first responding officer at the crime scene?

Q: There was the evidence custodian?

Q: The evidence custodian was responsible for maintaining the security of the evidence?

Q: There is you, the lead investigator?

Q: There was a medical examiner?

Q: There was an emergency room nurse?

Q: There was a forensic laboratory specialist?

Q: Anyone who handles physical evidence can affect that evidence?

Q: How evidence is handled can affect the integrity of the evidence?

Q: It is important that everyone who handles evidence in a case is trained in the proper procedures for handling evidence?

Q: Someone who does not know how to properly handle evidence should not handle evidence?

Q: Someone who does not have a legitimate need to handle evidence should not handle the evidence?

BASICS OF FORENSICS

Point: Physical evidence can make or break a sexual assault case.

Q: There are some types of evidence that are associated with sexual assaults?

Q: Depending on the circumstances of the case, any item in a crime scene can have value as evidence?

Q: The value of a piece of evidence can change as the investigation develops?

Q: For example, if a person had normal and regular access to a room that became a scene of a crime, finding that person's fingerprints in that room may not reveal significant information about the case?

Q: But, if a person's fingerprints are discovered in a place where that person denies they've been, those fingerprints can be important to the case?

Q: Analyzing evidence in a sexual assault case often involves comparing a known source with an unknown sample of evidence recovered from the crime scene?

Q: Physical evidence can make or break a sexual assault case?

Point: Forensic investigations match evidence to a source.

Q: Forensic investigation often involves identifying the source of a piece of evidence?

Q: Identifying a piece of evidence involves more than just simple observation?

Q: Evidence is often identified through scientific testing?

Q: For example, the source of blood can be identified through scientific testing?

Q: The source of semen can be identified through scientific testing?

Q: The source of hair can be identified through scientific testing?

Q: Testing evidence can provide information needed to distinguish one source of evidence from another?

Q: Testing evidence can also match a sample recovered from a crime scene to a known source?

Q: For example, you can match the DNA of a suspect to the DNA found at a crime scene?

Q: How a piece of evidence is identified depends on the type of evidence?

Q: It also depends on whether you have other sources, such as DNA, to compare it to?

Point: No class characteristic evidence was collected or tested, and it should have been.

Q: One type of evidence is called "class characteristic" evidence?

Q: Class characteristic evidence can't be matched to one specific source in a way that rules out other possible sources?

Q: This includes the non-DNA analysis of hairs, blood, saliva, or semen?

Q: This includes fibers?

Q: This includes soil?

Q: This includes glass?

Q: This includes wood particles?

Q: Forensic science can't match those kinds of evidence with a single source?

Q: So, in the analysis of class characteristic evidence, the goal is to get as much information as possible about each feature of the piece of evidence?

Q: By getting information on those features, an investigator can associate a suspect with a piece of class characteristic evidence?

Q: The more types of class characteristic evidence that the investigator can associate with a suspect, the stronger the association becomes?

116

Q: For example, one expert could testify that a hair from the suspect matches characteristics to a hair found on the victim's clothes?

Q: Another expert could testify that a fiber from the suspect's jacket matches characteristics to a fiber found on the victim's clothes?

Q: Meanwhile, another expert could testify that a liquid, such as body oil found in the suspect's car, matches characteristics to body oil found on the victim's body?

Q: Another expert may testify that soil found on a suspect's shoe matches the characteristics of soil found at the crime scene?

Q: By taking these pieces of evidence together, these associations can point to one suspect over another?

Q: Sometimes investigators overlook this type of evidence?

Q: Class characteristic evidence can often be found in abundance at a crime scene, if an investigator takes the time to look for it?

Q: Class characteristic evidence should not be ignored?

Q: In this case, no class characteristic evidence was collected from the crime scene?

Q: No fibers were collected?

Q: No hairs were collected?

Q: No dried substances were collected?

Q: No _____ were collected?

Q: In this case, no class characteristic evidence was sent to the forensic laboratory?

Q: In this case, no class characteristic evidence was tested?

Point: No individual characteristic evidence was collected or tested, and it should have been.

Q: One type of evidence is called "individual characteristic" evidence?

Q: Individual characteristic evidence can positively identify a specific source?

Q: It can also rule out all other sources?

Q: One example of individual characteristic evidence is DNA evidence?

117

Q: One example of individual characteristic evidence is fingerprints?

Q: Another example is specific cuts and tears in clothing?

Q: DNA can be positively identified with a specific source in a way that rules out all other sources?

Q: With individual characteristic evidence, the evidence conclusively matches?

Q: Often, individual characteristic evidence isn't as readily available at a crime scene than class characteristic evidence?

Q: Evidence that can establish that a particular person is the only source of the evidence is limited to only a few types of evidence?

Q: This includes latent fingerprints?

Q: This includes DNA?

Q: This includes bite marks through forensic dental comparisons?

Q: This includes handwriting or hand printing?

Q: Individual characteristic evidence may not even be found at the crime scene?

Q: Because of the rarity, it is unwise for an investigation to rely only on individual evidence if there's additional class evidence present?

Q: It is not uncommon for a piece of evidence to have individual and class characteristics?

Q: For example, if a victim wore a shirt that was torn during an assault in a suspect's vehicle: a piece of fabric taken from the vehicle could be compared with the shirt's color and fabric structure, and that would be class evidence?

Q: On the other hand, if semen was found on the shirt, then that semen could be tested for DNA?

Q: That DNA could then be compared with the suspect's DNA?

Q: The DNA on the shirt could be used to pinpoint a specific person as long as there were enough characteristics between the sample and the target person?

Q: This often depends on the quality and amount of the DNA sample?

Q: This type of evidence should not be ignored?

Q: In this case, no individual characteristic evidence was collected from the crime scene?

Q: No DNA was collected?

Q: No fingerprints were collected?

Q: No blood or semen were collected?

Q: No _____ were collected?

Q: In this case, no individual characteristic evidence was sent to the forensic laboratory?

Q: In this case, no individual characteristic evidence was tested?

TRANSFERENCE OF EVIDENCE

Point: Forensic evidence is easily transferred.

Q: Victims can bring pieces of evidence to a crime scene without even knowing it?

Q: Suspects can bring evidence to a crime scene without even knowing it?

Q: Law enforcement can bring evidence to a crime scene without even knowing it?

Q: People visiting the crime scene can bring evidence without even knowing it?

Q: Victims can take pieces of evidence away from a crime scene without even knowing it?

Q: Suspects can take pieces of evidence away from a crime scene without even knowing it?

Q: Law enforcement can take pieces of evidence away from a crime scene without even knowing it?

Q: People visiting the crime scene can take pieces of evidence away without even knowing it?

Q: This is called transfer evidence?

Q: Transfer evidence is left through contact?

Q: It is transferred by touching?

Q: Individuals often leave transfer evidence at crime scenes?

Q: Transfer evidence can include hairs?

Q: Transfer evidence can include fibers?

Q: Transfer evidence can include smears of semen?

Q: Transfer evidence can include smears of blood?

Q: Transfer evidence can include glass?

Q: Transfer evidence can include soils/plant matter?

Q: Transfer evidence is often found in very small amounts?

Q: Often, investigators need specialized lighting and other aids to find transfer evidence?

Q: Transfer evidence can be easily lost?

Q: Transfer evidence can offer information on how to reconstruct the events of the crime, depending on the kind of transfer evidence found?

Point: Trace evidence explained.

Q: At a crime scene, there are often tiny fragments of physical evidence that can help tell the story of what happened?

Q: Hairs, fibers from clothing or carpeting, or pieces of glass can help tell the story of what happened?

Q: These tiny fragments of physical evidence are called trace evidence?

Q: Trace evidence can be transferred when two objects touch?

Q: Trace evidence can become transfer evidence?

Q: Trace evidence can be transferred when small particles are disbursed by an action or movement?

Q: For example, paint can be transferred from one car to another in a collision?

Q: Or, a hair can be left on a sweater in a physical assault?

Q: This evidence can be used to reconstruct an event?

Q: This evidence can be used to prove that a person or thing was present?

Q: Careful collection of materials from a crime scene can yield a wealth of information about where a sample came from and how it helps to tell the story?

Q: Scientists examine the physical, optical, and chemical properties of trace evidence?

Q: Scientists can use a variety of tools to find and compare samples?

Q: Scientists can use tools to look for the source or origin of each item?

Q: Most test methods require magnification and/or chemical analysis?

Q: The importance of trace evidence in the context of crime scene investigation is sometimes understated?

Q: Trace evidence sometimes takes a back seat to more individualized evidence, such as DNA or fingerprints?

Q: Much can be learned about what happened at a scene through trace evidence?

Q: For example, trace evidence could determine whether an item or body was moved?

Q: For example, trace evidence could determine whether someone was assaulted from behind or from the side?

Q: Trace evidence can include a wide variety of materials?

Q: The most commonly tested are hair, fibers, paint and glass?

Q: Other, less frequently included items are soil, cosmetics, and fire debris?

Point: Direct transfer evidence explained.

Q: One kind of transfer evidence is called "direct transfer?"

Q: Direct transfer is when trace evidence transfers from the original source to another object?

Q: An example of direct transfer includes a bleeding person brushing against a tree at a crime scene, leaving blood on the tree?

Q: An example of direct transfer includes a suspect leaning against a wall with wet paint at a crime scene and getting paint on his shirt, or leaving fibers from his shirt in the paint?

Point: Indirect transfer evidence explained.

Q: A different kind of transfer evidence is called "indirect" or "secondary transfer?"

Q: Indirect transfer is when trace evidence is carried from a primary source to other sources by third persons or objects?

Q: An example of indirect transfer might be if wet paint from a wall at the crime scene ends up on a suspect's shirt, and then chips of paint fall off the shirt and end up in the suspect's car?

Q: The identification of indirect transfer can indicate the need to expand an investigation to other areas besides the original crime scene?

Q: It is important to preserve and document any kind of trace evidence when it is identified?

Q: Trace evidence transferred to one location can be transferred again?

Q: For example, a person can transfer DNA from one location to another, then that same DNA can be transferred again?

Q: If trace evidence isn't properly protected and preserved, it can be lost?

Point: Investigators must evaluate all evidence at the crime scene.

Q: Reconstructing a crime scene involves understanding a concept called the "evidence environment?"

Q: The evidence environment refers to the crime scene and the unique characteristics and combinations of evidence that make up the crime scene?

Q: By being knowledgeable of those characteristics and combinations, an investigator can better spot trace evidence common to both the scene and the suspect?

Q: The evidence environment approach provides several guidelines of crime scene investigation?

Q: One of those guidelines is that evidence made up of unique or uncommon materials can be valuable?

Q: Evidence sources that are extremely common provide very little evidentiary value because they are so common?

Q: For example, grains of sand found at a beach crime scene might not be relevant because they are so common?

Q: Meanwhile, green grass found at a beach crime scene might be highly significant?

Q: Class characteristic evidence is significant when there are multiple samples that can be matched from the scene to the suspect?

Q: With trace evidence, the evidence environment concept tells us that the more transfers that take place, the stronger the association is between the original source and the person or object receiving the transferred material?

Q: Greater amounts of transfer evidence can indicate more contact between one source and another?

Q: Failure to employ the evidence environment concept in an investigation can result in flaws in the investigation?

Q: For example, a failure to categorize items normally present in the assault scene as known samples can prevent a forensic technician from connecting recovered fibers to the suspect?

Q: This is because forensic science involves the study of comparisons between known and unknown samples?

Q: A lack of known reference samples makes a forensic examiner's job more difficult?

CONTAMINATION AND DESTRUCTION OF EVIDENCE

Point: Contamination of evidence can jeopardize a criminal case.

Q: Contamination of evidence can be a serious problem?

Q: Contamination of evidence can ruin evidence?

Q: Contamination of evidence can jeopardize a criminal case?

Q: Contamination occurs when something is introduced into the scene that was not previously there?

Q: Most contamination comes from the people investigating the scene?

Q: Evaluating a scene before anyone enters can be key to keeping contamination to a minimum?

Q: Various people can contaminate the evidence at a crime scene?

Q: Witnesses can contaminate the evidence at a crime scene?

Q: Suspects can contaminate the evidence at a crime scene?

Q: Innocent bystanders can contaminate the evidence at a crime scene?

Q: A victim can contaminate the evidence at a crime scene?

Q: First responders can contaminate the evidence at a crime scene?

Q: Police officers can contaminate the evidence at a crime scene?

Q: Crime scene investigators can contaminate the evidence at a crime scene?

Q: One of the most important ways to limit contamination is by limiting access to the scene?

Q: Evidence can get contaminated at various stages of the investigation?

Q: Evidence can be contaminated at the crime scene?

Q: Evidence can be contaminated on the way to the laboratory?

Q: Evidence can be contaminated in the laboratory?

Q: Because of that risk, it is the responsibility of everyone who handles the evidence to guard against contamination?

Point: Contamination of evidence must be documented.

Q: Crime scenes are often disorganized environments?

Q: There is a chance that pieces of evidence may become contaminated in a crime scene?

Q: When information regarding contamination of evidence is discovered, it needs to be documented?

Q: If not properly documented, then contaminated evidence could mislead investigators?

Q: If not properly documented, then contaminated evidence could mislead forensic scientists?

Q: Contamination of evidence can jeopardize a criminal case?

Point: Anyone who comes into contact with a crime scene is capable of contaminating it.

Q: Anyone who enters a crime scene is capable of accidentally adding something to the scene?

Q: Anyone who enters a crime scene is capable of accidentally removing something from the scene?

Q: Anyone at the crime scene is capable of contaminating the scene?

Q: Because of this, it is better to limit the number of people who enter the scene?

Q: If someone doesn't have a legitimate purpose in investigating the scene, they should not be allowed on the scene?

Q: Those who have a legitimate purpose in being at the crime scene should be aware of their potential to contaminate the scene?

Q: Any clothing that could add or remove trace evidence should be avoided?

Q: In this case, no policies or procedures were put into place to avoid contamination of the scene?

Point: Carelessness at the scene can alter or destroy evidence.

Q: Persons who are careless in working at a crime scene can alter or even destroy evidence before it is collected?

Q: Persons who are untrained in working at a crime scene can alter or even destroy evidence before it is collected?

Q: Because of this, it is important to limit crime scene access of personnel who have no need to be there?

Q: Because of this, it is important to limit crime scene access to trained personnel?

Point: Improperly packaged and stored evidence can result in contamination.

Q: There are specific procedures for recovering evidence from a crime scene?

Q: Those procedures involve marking the item?

Q: After the item is marked, it should be packaged properly?

Q: The container the evidence is placed in should be sealed?

Q: It should not be removed from the original packaging before laboratory personnel examine it?

Q: The container should also be marked as to the identity of the item inside?

Q: The container should mark the location where the evidence was found?

Q: The container should mark the date the evidence was found?

Q: The container should mark the time the evidence was recovered?

Q: The container should mark the name of the person who collected it?

Q: If forensic personnel open an evidence container before its examination, the contents can become contaminated?

Q: Tiny fragments of physical evidence are called trace evidence?

Q: Trace evidence can be transferred when an action or movement disburses small particles?

Q: Trace evidence can also be lost if the container is improperly opened?

Q: If the container is improperly opened, it also makes it difficult to tell what the precise source of trace evidence found on the evidence item is?

Q: Opening an evidence container prematurely can compromise the evidence?

Q: Packaging materials should also protect the evidence against damage?

Q: Improper packaging can also contaminate the evidence?

Q: Some cardboard containers can have residual cardboard dust from manufacturing?

Q: Some plastic vials can contaminate chemical evidence?

Q: Evidence packaging left unprotected in a vehicle for too long can collect contaminants from the vehicle?

Q: Improperly packaging a piece of evidence can also result in contaminating the evidence when it is opened at the lab?

Point: The environment can rapidly degrade evidence.

Q: Evidence can degrade?

Q: A significant amount of sexual assault evidence involves bodily fluids?

Q: That includes blood?

Q: That includes saliva?

Q: That includes vaginal mucus?

Q: That includes semen?

Q: The biochemistry of body fluids is fragile?

Q: The biochemistry of body fluids is more fragile when it comes to hostile environments?

Q: Influences from the environment can rapidly degrade evidence?

Q: Heat can rapidly degrade evidence?

Q: Humidity can rapidly degrade evidence?

Point: Heat can degrade body fluid evidence.

Q: Heat can degrade body fluid evidence?

Q: Because of this, sexual assault evidence should be stored in a cool environment?

Q: Often, that means using a refrigerator?

Q: This is particularly important for blood samples?

Q: It is routine practice to store sexual assault evidence in refrigerators or freezers?

Point: Humidity can rapidly degrade evidence

Q: Wet evidence should be dried as soon as possible after it is recovered?

Q: Blood should be dried as soon as possible after it is recovered?

Q: Semen should be dried as soon as possible after it is recovered?

Q: Saliva should be dried as soon as possible after it is recovered?

Q: Vaginal secretions should be dried as soon as possible after they are recovered?

Q: If the evidence is allowed to remain moist, bacteria can grow inside the evidence?

Q: If this happens, the bacteria can degrade the substances laboratory analysts use to identify the evidence?

Q: Packaging wet evidence in plastic bags can accelerate the degradation of the evidence?

Q: Packaging wet evidence in airtight containers can accelerate the degradation of the evidence?

Q: Packaging wet evidence speeds up the degradation of the evidence?

Q: If this happens, the evidence may be useless before it reaches the laboratory?

Point: UV light can degrade body fluid evidence.

Q: Ultraviolet light can degrade substances in body fluids, like DNA?

Q: Samples that contain DNA should be protected from UV sources?

Q: Sources of UV radiation include direct sunlight?

Q: Alternate light sources, like black lights used in crime scene investigation, can generate UV light?

Q: Black lights used in hospital emergency rooms to help locate sexual assault evidence can also generate UV light?

Q: Prolonged exposure to UV light can damage the chemical integrity of the DNA evidence?

Point: Victims can destroy evidence.

Q: The victim's body is considered a crime scene in a sexual assault investigation?

Q: Victims are often emotionally distraught following a sexual assault?

Q: The victim might take steps to distance themselves from the assault experience?

Q: This might include actions like bathing?

Q: The victim might change clothes?

Q: The victim might even destroy the clothes they wore during the assault?

Q: The victim might refuse to tell others about the assault?

Q: The victim might refuse to reveal more sensitive details of the assault, like oral or anal penetration, to investigators?

Q: If a victim takes some of these actions, they can destroy or limit the recoverable evidence from the victim?

Q: For example, evidence like blood, semen, or hairs can be lost because of a shower, or in a clothes washer?

Q: When a victim makes contact with the authorities, it is important that the authorities preserve potential evidence?

Q: The victim should be counseled to avoid taking actions that might damage the integrity and preservation of the evidence?

Q: Often, the victim is taken to a hospital for examination and collection of evidence?

Q: When the victim is taken to a hospital, they should be instructed to bring an extra change of clothes?

Q: This is so the clothes worn during the assault can be taken as evidence?

Q: The victim may have to change clothes before they are transported to the hospital?

Q: In cases like this, the victim should disrobe over a clean white cloth or paper?

Q: This helps to preserve trace evidence?

Q: Each item of clothing should be packaged separately?

Q: The paper or cloth should be marked to identify the side facing the victim?

Q: Then it should be folded to retain any trace evidence that was dislodged while the victim undressed?

Q: It is preferable to do this at a hospital rather than at the scene?

Q: Before evidence is collected from the victim, photographs should be taken?

Q: The recovery of evidence from the victim should be done while wearing gloves?

Q: This helps to avoid contamination?

Q: DNA analysis, for instance, can be affected by residue from the skin of the person collecting the evidence?

Q: If the victim is taken to a hospital for evidence collection and examination, it is important that the investigators coordinate with medical personnel about handling evidence?

Q: Sometimes when a victim is seriously injured, medical personnel cut the clothing off the victim to allow for fast treatment?

Q: If this happens, the removal of the clothing should be documented as best as possible?

Q: The clothing should be packaged and collected as soon as possible?

Q: Without documentation, forensic examiners won't know if hospital personnel or the suspect cut the victim's clothing?

Point: Suspects can destroy evidence.

Q: In a sexual assault investigation, the suspect's body is considered a crime scene?

Q: Before a suspect can be examined for evidence, the suspect first has to be identified?

Q: The longer it takes to identify a suspect, the greater the chance for evidence from the suspect to be lost?

Q: Clothing may be discarded?

Q: Vehicles may be cleaned?

Q: The suspect may bathe him or herself?

Q: The suspect may change their appearance?

Q: Suspects identified shortly after an assault are more likely to have valuable evidence associated with them?

Q: If an extended period passes after the assault before the suspect is identified, it is possible that most of the evidence will be lost from the suspect's body?

Q: In situations like this, trace evidence should not be overlooked?

Q: Trace evidence like hairs?

Q: Trace evidence like fibers?

Q: Trace evidence like soil?

Q: The presence of disease may also be a manner of associating a suspect with a victim?

Q: When a victim develops symptoms of a sexually transmitted disease as a result of the assault, investigators should determine the medical condition of the suspect?

Q: Even if an extended period of time passes between the assault and the identification of the suspect, investigators should still collect evidence from the suspect?

Point: Evidence collection kits must be properly used.

Q: One role of physical evidence in sexual assault crimes is to link the victim, suspect, and the crime scene?

Q: Another role of the physical evidence is to show that sexual contact in fact took place?

Q: Both of these roles are established in forensic science by comparing known samples of evidence with unknown samples collected from the scene?

Q: Collecting samples of evidence from the victim and the suspect can be critical to the investigation?

Q: One tool for collecting those samples is a sexual assault evidence collection kit?

Q: Law enforcement and medical personnel who deal with sexual assaults have access to these kits?

Q: These kits are designed to be relatively easy to use?

Q: These kits often provide procedures for effectively collecting evidence?

Q: In order to use these kits properly, the personnel have to be properly trained?

Q: Improperly trained personnel can mishandle the evidence?

Q: Mishandled evidence can produce inconclusive test results?

Q: Part of making sure that evidence is not mishandled involves using procedures for proper chain of custody?

Q: Sexual assault kits have materials for properly documenting the evidence collected?

Q: These documents guide the examination and interview of the victim?

Q: These documents include chain of custody records to track what evidence was collected?

Q: Using these forms allows for the proper collection of evidence?

Q: During the examination of the victim, the examiner should ask the victim about recent consensual sexual activity?

Q: If the victim has had recent consensual sexual activity, a blood sample may have to be secured from the victim's partner?

Q: This will allow investigators to eliminate any DNA results the partner may have contributed to the evidence?

Q: During evidence collection using a sexual assault evidence kit, all containers should be properly marked and identified?

Q: Attention to detail is important?

Q: This includes documenting where the evidence came from?

Q: The name of the person packaging the evidence should be documented?

Q: The time and date of the collection should be documented?

Q: The location of the examination should be documented?

Q: When swabs or fluids are used as part of a sexual assault evidence collection kit, the examiner should provide an unused or uncontaminated swab or fluid sample for control purposes?

Q: When a comb or brush is provided to collect hair, for example, the hair is brushed over a clean cloth or paper to catch any loose hairs or fibers?

Q: The comb itself should also be packaged with the materials collected?

Q: When a kit allows for collection of fingernail scrapings, each hand should be done separately and packaged separately?

Q: In using evidence collection kits, there are several guidelines examiners should be mindful of?

Q: While the pubic region of the victim is often examined, it is important to also examine the hair on the victim's head for trace evidence?

Q: Because some victims are reluctant to discuss oral or anal penetration, sampling of those areas should often be performed as normal policy?

Q: The failure to use catch papers or cloths can result in the loss of trace evidence?

OVERLOOKED FORENSIC EVIDENCE

Point: Investigators should not ignore potential sources of evidence.

Q: The investigation of a crime scene has become more complex and sensitive than it was decades ago?

Q: The value of evidence collected from a crime scene is often linked to the level of care exercised in collecting that evidence?

Q: Sloppy collection or documentation can mean that evidence is lost?

Q: It can mean that evidence is useless for forensic examination?

Q: Well-designed protocols for evidence collection can make a major difference in the effectiveness of the evidence collected?

Q: Crime scene investigation should be looked at as a step-by-step process?

Q: Carefully following those steps allows for the job to be done correctly?

Q: In a sexual assault investigation, the assault scene, the victim, and the suspect are all crime scenes?

Q: The investigation should not focus on one scene at the expense of giving the other scenes the proper attention?

Q: Failing to pay attention to all potential sources of evidence can be disastrous for an investigation?

DNA EVIDENCE

Point: DNA transfers easily.

Q: I want to talk with you about DNA transfer, okay?

A: Yes.

Q: Are you familiar with that concept?

A: Yes.

Q: DNA can transfer from a person to an object?

A: Yes.

Q: DNA can transfer from a person to another person?

A: Yes.

Q: For example, if a person drips semen onto a pillowcase in a bedroom, his DNA transfers from inside his body onto the pillowcase?

A: Yes.

Q: That is called primary transfer?

A: Yes.

Q: If someone's hand touched the semen on the pillowcase, then some of the semen could transfer from the pillowcase to the hand?

A: Yes.

Q: That is called secondary transfer?

A: Yes.

Q: Now, if the person with the semen on their hand walked to an upstairs bathroom and wiped their hands on a hand towel, then some of the semen could transfer from the hand to the towel?

A: Yes.

Q: That is called tertiary transfer?

A: Yes.

Q: Because of these types of transfers, you can find semen in a room in which the source of the semen was never present?

A: Yes.

Q: Other forms of DNA can transfer the same way?

A: Yes.

Q: For example, if a person was cut, blood could transfer from their body to the floor?

A: Yes.

Q: That blood would contain their DNA?

A: Yes.

Q: Then, someone wearing shoes could step in the wet blood?

A: Yes.

Q: The DNA in the blood would now be on the shoe?

A: Yes.

Q: If that person walked into another room, they could transfer the blood from their shoe to other areas?

A: Yes.

Q: In another example, skin cells containing my DNA can transfer from my hands to your hands?

A: Yes.

Q: If we shook hands?

A: Yes.

Q: If you then went and grabbed a book, while my DNA was still on your hands, you could potentially transfer my DNA to the book?

A: Yes.

Q: Even if I never touched the book?

A: Yes.

Point: A major DNA profile provides limited information when multiple factors are present.

....

Q: People can transfer DNA onto clothes they are wearing?

A: Yes.

Q: For example, you would expect to find your DNA on the underwear you are wearing right now?

A: Yes.

Q: You would expect to find my DNA on the socks I am wearing right now?

A: Yes.

Q: This type of DNA is called wearer DNA?

A: Yes.

Q: If I put on your underwear right now, my DNA would transfer to the underwear as well?

A: Yes.

Q: The underwear would then have my DNA profile and your DNA profile?

A: Yes.

Q: Some people shed, or leave behind, more DNA than others?

A: Yes.

Q: Skin cells contain DNA?

A: Yes.

Q: People shed their skin cells at different rates?

A: Yes.

Q: People shed their DNA at different rates?

A: Yes.

Q: Some people shed skin cells much faster than others?

A: Yes.

Q: For example, I may shed skin cells twice as fast as you?

A: Yes.

Q: In your report, it says that more than one DNA profile was found?

A: Yes.

Q: The DNA of at least two people was found?

A: Yes.

Q: In your report, you use the term "major profile?"

A: Yes.

Q: The major DNA profile refers to the person who has more DNA than the other person?

A: Yes.

Q: Using the underwear example. If we both wore the underwear, and both of our DNA was found on the underwear, whichever one of us left behind the most DNA would be called the major profile?

A: Yes.

Q. The term major DNA profile does not tell us who wore the clothing first?

A: No.

Q: The term major DNA profile does not tell us who wore the clothing last?

A: No.

Q: The term major DNA profile does not tell us who wore the clothing the longest?

A: No.

Q: The term major DNA profile does not tell us who wore the clothing the most often?

A: No.

Q: What it tells us is that the person with the major DNA profile may have had contact with that item at some point in time?

A: Yes.

Q: The term major DNA profile does not tell us when the contact occurred?

A: Correct.

Q: The term major DNA profile does not tell us where the contact occurred?

A: Correct.

Q: The term major DNA profile does not tell us how the contact occurred?

A: Correct.

Point: DNA testing does not prove how, when, or where the DNA was deposited.

Q: DNA testing does not tell us what time the DNA was deposited?

A: Correct.

Q: DNA testing does not tell us the date the DNA was deposited?

A: Correct.

Q: DNA testing does not tell us when any of the DNA was deposited?

A: Correct.

Q: The DNA testing does not tell us whether the DNA was deposited consensually?

A: Yes.

DNA EVIDENCE HANDLING PROCEDURES

Point: Law enforcement should not open sealed sexual assault kits.

Q: In this case, there were sexual assault kits collected from both the accused and the alleged victim?

Q: These are white cardboard boxes?

Q: The boxes contained envelopes with swabs?

Q: The boxes contained other evidence collected by the forensic nurse?

Q: It is your understanding that once the nurse collects this evidence, the box is sealed?

Q: Then the box is turned over to law enforcement agents?

Q: The law enforcement agents then submit the evidence to your laboratory for testing?

Q: Would you agree that law enforcement should not open the kits the nurse collected?

138

Q: Would you agree that law enforcement should not open the envelopes and swab boxes inside the kits the nurse collected?

Q: Especially before they send the kits to the DNA lab for testing?

Q: The main reason why law enforcement should not open the evidence prior to sending it to your laboratory for testing is because they could comprise the integrity of the evidence?

Q: Meaning, they could cause cross-contamination between different evidence items or even contaminate the evidence themselves?

Q: They could even contaminate the evidence itself?

Q: Especially if they did not take the proper precautions when opening and handling the evidence?

Q: Such as using gloves?

Q: Changing gloves before examining each item of evidence?

Q: Cleaning the table they are using before examining each item?

Q: Wearing protective gear, such as goggles?

Q: Wearing a surgical mask to prevent saliva or DNA from their mouth and face from coming into contact with evidence?

Q: Wearing a medical cap or similar item to prevent their hairs from being deposited on the evidence?

Q: Now, you received the sexual assault kits from the accused and the alleged victim?

Q: Did you open the kits and test the evidence at your desk?

Q: Did you open the kits and test the evidence in the conference room at the lab?

DNA LAB DID NOT RECEIVE KEY EVIDENCE FROM LAW ENFORCEMENT

In many cases, investigators selectively choose what evidence they will send to the lab for forensic testing. They usually only submit and request testing on items that will help build the case for the prosecution. If evidence is likely to exculpate the accused or cast doubt on the alleged victims story, then the agents will sometimes not submit these items to the lab. They will declare them irrelevant. The defense lawyer must highlight this practice to the jury, and show that investigators failed to submit crucial evidence, evidence which could show the accused's innocence, to the lab for testing.

Point: Law enforcement did not submit crucial evidence for testing.

Q: Your lab did not receive the accused's underwear?

Q: If you had received the underwear, you could have tested them for DNA?

Q: For example, if the alleged victim had put her hand down into the accused's underwear to touch his penis, her skin cells and DNA could have transferred to his penis?

Q: Her skin cells and DNA could have transferred to his underwear because she physically touched them?

Q: Your lab did not receive the comforter from the bed in the alleged victim's room?

Q: However, if you had received her comforter, you could have examined and tested it for body fluids and DNA?

Q: For example, if there was a question of whether or not the accused had actually been on the bed, testing the comforter for forensic evidence may have helped answer this question?

Q: If there was a question of whether or not he had been on a specific area of the bed, testing the comforter for forensic evidence may have helped answer this question?

Q: Your lab did not receive fingernail scrapings from the alleged victim?

Q: These fingernail scrapings are normally collected during the hospital examination and included in the kit?

Q: Fingernail scrapings are collected from someone because if they scratched another person during an assault or struggle, these scrapings could contain blood, tissue, and DNA of the assailant?

Q: Your lab did not receive the alleged victim's sweatpants she was wearing that night?

Q: However, if you had received her sweatpants, you could have tested them for DNA?

Q: If the accused had forcefully pulled the sweatpants off her body, he would have touched the waist area of her sweatpants with his bare hands and transferred his skin cells there?

Q: You could have tested these skin cells for his DNA?

Q: And if the accused's DNA was not found on the waist area of her sweatpants, that could mean he never actually touched her sweatpants or removed them from her body?

EVIDENCE THE DNA LAB RECEIVED BUT DID NOT EXAMINE

In a case where DNA evidence may determine the outcome of the trial, the defense must show the DNA laboratory did not examine all relevant evidence. In particular, the defense should highlight the pieces of evidence the lab chose to not examine that was potentially exculpatory.

Point: Lab did not examine potentially exculpatory evidence.

Q: You received the bed sheets from the alleged victim's room?

Q: But you did not examine or perform any testing on her bed sheets?

Q: Again, like the bed comforter we discussed earlier, you could have tested the bed sheets for body fluids and DNA?

Q: Which could have been helpful in determining if the accused was actually in the bed or at a specific location on the bed?

Q: And if none of his hairs or body fluids or DNA were on the bed sheets, then one could conclude he was never in the bed?

Q: You received the accused's pubic hair combings?

Q: These were collected during his hospital examination?

Q: These were included in his kit?

Q: One purpose of these combings is to recover any pubic hairs originating from a female he might have had sex with?

Q: Because during sexual intercourse, the pubic hairs from the male and female can become mixed together?

Q: One type of testing that could have been done would be to search the accused's pubic hair combings for any pubic hairs that were not his?

Q: That would include microscopic examinations of the combings?

Q: The trace evidence laboratory could have done this?

Q: This could have been done by another government forensic laboratory?

Q: A private forensic laboratory could have done this?

Q: If any foreign pubic hairs were found in the accused's pubic hair combings, DNA testing could have been performed on those foreign hairs to determine who the hairs came from?

Q: If there were roots on those foreign pubic hairs, you could have done DNA testing on those hair roots?

Q: Briefly explain to the jury what hair roots are?

Q: Now, if there were no roots on the foreign pubic hairs found in the accused's pubic hair combings, you could have sent the hairs to a laboratory that performs mitochondrial DNA testing?

Q: You can get mitochondrial DNA out of hairs that have no roots?

Q: Besides microscopic examinations and mitochondrial DNA testing, you could have swabbed the accused's pubic hairs and tested those swabs for DNA?

Q: If the accused had sexual intercourse with the alleged victim, his pubic hairs would have her vaginal secretions on them?

Q: If the accused had sexual intercourse with the alleged victim, his pubic hairs would have her skin cells on them?

Q: If the accused had sexual intercourse with the alleged victim, his pubic hairs would have her DNA done on them?

Q: In this case, no microscopic examinations were done on the accused's pubic hairs by your DNA laboratory?

Q: No microscopic examinations were done on the accused's pubic hairs by the trace evidence laboratory?

Q: No microscopic examinations were done on the accused's pubic hairs by any other forensic laboratory?

Q: In this case, no DNA testing was done on the accused's pubic hairs by your DNA laboratory?

Q: In this case, no DNA testing was done on the accused's pubic hairs by the trace evidence laboratory?

Q: In this case, no DNA testing was done on the accused's pubic hairs by any other forensic laboratory?

STANDARD CROSS FOR SEROLOGY AND DNA TESTING

During the cross examination of the prosecution's DNA expert, the defense must show the jury why the DNA evidence does not prove that a sexual assault occurred.

Q: You tested the alleged victim's vaginal swabs?

Q: You tested the alleged victim's perineal swabs?

Q: You tested the alleged victim's panties?

Q: The perineal swabs were collected from the skin area between her vagina and anus?

Q: You did not find any blood on any of the swabs?

Q: You did not find any blood on any of the swabs on her panties?

Q: If there had been any trauma to her vagina or perineum that caused bleeding, you could find blood on her vaginal swabs?

Q: If there had been bleeding, you could find blood on her perineal swabs?

Q: If there had been bleeding, you could find blood on her panties?

Q: You did not find any semen on her vaginal swabs?

Q: You did not find any semen on her perineal swabs?

Q: You did not find any semen on her panties?

Q: The three semen tests you used would also give a positive result if pre-ejaculate was on these items?

Q: Pre-ejaculate is the fluid that is discharged from the urethra of a man's penis during initial sexual arousal and foreplay?

Q: And pre-ejaculate can contain sperm and seminal fluid proteins that you test for?

Q: But you found no semen or sperm on her vaginal swabs, perineal swabs, or panties?

Q: Because you did not find any semen, no DNA testing was performed on the alleged victim's vaginal swabs, perineal swabs, or panties?

Q: However, since it is alleged that the accused had sexual intercourse with the alleged victim, you could have tested the vaginal swabs, perineal swabs, and panties using Y-STR testing?

Q: Y-STR testing is DNA testing that only detects male DNA?

Q: Your DNA laboratory has the capability of performing Y-STR testing?

Q: It is actually part of your Standard Operating Procedures Manual?

Q: Regarding the alleged victim's panties, you could have tested the waist area of her panties for DNA?

Q: If the accused had forcefully pulled her panties off her body, he would have touched the waist area of her underwear with his bare hands and transferred his skin cells there?

Q: You could have tested these skin cells for his DNA?

Q: If the accused's DNA was not found on the waist area of her panties, that could mean he never actually touched her underwear?

Q: That could mean he never removed them from her body?

Q: You tested the alleged victim's buccal swabs for semen?

Q: These buccal swabs were collected from inside her mouth?

Q: The swabs were negative for the accused's DNA?

Q: Now, you tested the accused's penile swabs and did not find any semen?

Q: So, one conclusion from that test result could be that he never ejaculated?

Q: It could also mean that no pre-ejaculate was on his penis?

Q: You performed DNA testing on the accused's penile swab?

Q: Your report states that the alleged victim's DNA was found on his penile swab?

Q: This DNA would be from her skin cells?

Q: But you cannot tell us exactly where these skin cells came from on her body?

Q: Her DNA could have come from her mouth?

Q: For example, if she was performing oral sex on him?

Q: Her DNA could have come from her hands?

Q: For example, if she was rubbing his penis with her hands?

Q: You don't know if the DNA on his penis came from sexual intercourse?

Q: You cannot tell us with any scientific certainty that the DNA on his penile swab is from her vaginal secretions?

Q: You cannot tell us with any scientific certainty that the DNA on his penile swab is from sexual intercourse?

Q: The DNA on his penile swab could be from the skin cells on her hand, or any part of her own body fluids that may have been on her hand?

Q: For example, if the alleged victim put her hand down his pants and rubbed his penis with her hand, her skin cells and DNA would be transferred to his penis?

Q: That scenario could certainly explain how her DNA got on his penis?

ADDITIONAL CROSS EXAMINATION OF THE DNA EXAMINER

The DNA examiner might say the amount of female DNA on the penile swab could only be from vaginal fluid or secretion, and not from hand-penis contact.

Point: There are many other scenarios that could account for the amount of female DNA on the penile swab.

Q: You don't know if the alleged victim had some fluid or secretion on her hand at the time she put it on the accused's penis?

Q: Sweat can transfer DNA?

Q: Sweat could have been on her hand?

Q: You cannot rule out that scenario?

Q: Vaginal secretions can transfer DNA?

Q: Vaginal secretions could have been on her hand?

Q: You cannot rule out that scenario?

Q: Saliva can transfer DNA?

Q: Saliva could have been on her hand?

Q: You cannot rule out that scenario?

Q: You do not know what fluids were on her hand when she touched my client's penis?

Q: People shed skin cells at different rates?

Q: The average person is shedding hundreds of thousands of skin cells per day?

Q: It is possible that the amount of female DNA on the penile swab could be from the alleged victim rubbing his penis?

Q: This is especially true if she sheds skin cells rapidly?

Q: You cannot rule out that scenario?

Point: DNA examiners cannot vouch for the integrity of the evidence before they received it.

Q: You cannot vouch for the integrity of the evidence before you received it?

Q: You do not know how the evidence was handled before you received it?

Q: You do not know how the evidence was collected before you received it?

WHEN THE DNA LAB DOES NOT TEST ALL ITEMS

This cross came from a case where the accused allegedly raped an El Salvadorian housekeeper. The investigators collected 17 pieces of evidence and then only tested select pieces.

Point: The DNA lab selectively tested evidence.

Q: You testified that you received more items than just the bra?

A: Yes, I did.

Q: In total, you said you received 17 pieces of evidence?

A: Yes, that's accurate. A little bit more because some are broken down into sub exhibits but 17 total containers of evidence.

Q: So you received 17 different containers of evidence?

A: Yes.

Q: Each container contained multiple pieces of evidence?

A: More or less.

Q: Each container contained multiple pieces of evidence?

A: Yes.

Q: There was over 39 pieces of evidence contained in the containers?

A: I think that's right.

Q: That is what it says in your report, 39 pieces, correct?

A: Yes, that is accurate.

Q: Of the 39 different pieces of evidence you received, how many did you test?

A: Not all the items that were submitted were analyzed.

Q: Of the 39 items, how many did you test?

A: I'm not sure.

Q: What specific items from the sexual assault kit did you test?

A: I examined a blood standard from the sexual assault kit from the accused. I examined a sample that was collected from a mattress top. I also examined an article of clothing that was collected from the victim. I also examined the bedding, a flat sheet, a fitted sheet, a pillow case, as well as a Kleenex tissue that was obtained from the residence.

Q: Of the 39 pieces of evidence, you tested 7?

A: Well, I didn't think it was necessary to test them all.

Q: You tested 7 of 39 pieces of evidence?

A: Well, we generally look for the best items to test.

147

Q: You tested 7 of 39?

A: Yes, that's correct.

Q: You tested a flat sheet?

A: Yes.

Q: You also tested a fitted sheet?

A: Yes.

Q: You tested a pillowcase?

A: Yes.

Q: No semen was found on the sheets?

A: There was minimal staining that was observed with the poly light and the subsequent analysis of those sheets, and I was not able to detect any semen.

Q: You found no semen on the flat sheet?

A: No.

Q: You found no semen on the fitted sheet?

A: No.

Q: You also tested a pillowcase?

A: I think the pillowcase came from the bed where the alleged assault occurred?

Q: You also tested a pillowcase?

A: Yes.

Q: The pillowcase was burgundy color?

A: There were two different areas that encompassed three very small stains.

Q: The pillowcase was burgundy color?

A: Yes.

Q: The pillowcase had two areas with stains?

A: Yes.

Q: Within those two areas, there were additional smaller stains?

A: Yes.

Q: You tested all of the stains on the pillowcase?

A: Yes.

Q: You tested the big stains?

A: Yes.

Q: You tested the small stains?

A: Yes.

Q: Not one of the stains on the pillowcase tested positive for semen?

A: That's correct.

Q: Before testifying here today, you reviewed the case file?

A: Yes.

Q: You read the statement of the alleged victim?

A: Yes.

Q: You also listened to her testimony here in this court martial?

A: Yes.

Q: The alleged victim claimed she had semen on her chest?

A: Yes.

Q: On her face?

A: Yes.

Q: In her hair?

A: Yes.

Q: She also claimed she wiped her face with the burgundy pillowcase?

A: Yes.

Q: She claimed she wiped her chest with the burgundy pillowcase?

A: Yes.

Q: She claimed she wiped her hair with the burgundy pillowcase?

A: Yes.

Q: She said she used the pillowcase to wipe off the semen?

A: Yes.

Q: If she wiped her face, chest, and hair with the pillowcase, you would expect there would be a transfer of the DNA to the pillowcase?

A: Well, I'm not sure. I cannot say.

Q: If she used the pillowcase to wipe wet semen off her hair, would you not expect that some semen would transfer to the pillowcase?

A: If the semen was still in a liquid form, potentially yes, you could get a transfer.

Q: Wet semen would have transferred to the pillowcase?

A: Well, I cannot say for sure.

Q: Under what circumstances would wet semen not transfer to the pillow case, if the wet semen was deliberately wiped on the pillowcase?

A: I don't know.

Q: Can you imagine a situation where some semen, even a tiny amount, would not transfer?

A: If it was dry.

Q: But here it was wet; it was fresh. The only circumstance you can imagine is if it was dry?

A: I mean… I don't know.

Q: Can you imagine a situation where wet semen, even a tiny amount, would not transfer?

A: I can't think of one.

Q: Semen does not dry the instant it hits the air?

A: No.

Q: It is not like fast drying super glue, where it dries in a few seconds?

A: No.

Q: And if there was semen on the chest, and she used the pillowcase to wipe her chest, would you expect there to be transfer of the DNA to the pillowcase?

A: Once again, if it was still wet, it would be fair to say you could potentially get a transfer.

Q: And the same with the face? If she used the pillowcase to wipe the wet semen from her face, you would expect there to be transfer of the DNA to the pillowcase?

A: Yes, that's correct.

Q: Given the absence of semen and DNA on the pillowcase, it is possible that she never wiped the semen on the pillowcase?

A: Yes, that's possible.

Point: DNA is transferred by contact.

Q: DNA can be transferred when two objects come into contact with one another?

150

A: Yes.

Q: Moist or wet DNA transfers more easily than dry DNA?

A: Usually, yes.

Q: In this case, if the complaining witness had used the sheets to clean her face, or her chest, or her hair, which she claimed had semen on it, you would expect to find the DNA on the sheets?

A: There would be a possibility that I could find it.

Q: You tested these areas because you expected to find DNA?

A: Not necessarily.

Q: You selected 7 out of 39 items to test?

A: Yes.

Q: You then located stains on these items?

A: Yes.

Q: You then tested the stains on these items?

A: Yes.

Q: You tested these areas specifically looking for DNA?

A: Yes.

Q: You were looking for the DNA of the accused?

A: Yes.

Q: You were looking for the DNA of the alleged victim?

A: Yes.

Q: You were looking for semen?

A: Yes.

Q: On the sheets alone, you found 13 different stains?

A: The fitted sheet had a total of seven different areas that fluoresced that I tested. And they were more congregated towards the center of the sheet. And each one of those stains was negative for semen. The flat sheet had a total of six stains, and they were more along the edges of the sheet itself. And once again, all six of those stains were negative for semen.

Q: Of the 13 stains, there was no semen?

A: None was identified.

Q: If semen was there, and you tested it, you would have identified it?

A: Most likely, yes.

Q: Of the 13 stains, there was no semen?

A: Not that I found.

Q: Are you saying there were semen stains, and you as an expert forensic scientist failed to find it?

A: No, I'm just saying we didn't find it.

Q: On the pillowcase you didn't find any semen?

A: That is correct. No semen was identified.

Q: The alleged victim said she was bleeding profusely from her vagina?

A: She said there was a lot of blood.

Q: She said there was a lot of blood coming out of her vagina?

A: I believe that is what she said.

Q: She said it was everywhere?

A: Yes. It was coming out.

Q: She said it was on the sheets?

A: Yes.

Q: She said it was on her clothes?

A: Yes.

Q: She said it was on the pillowcase?

A: Yes.

Q: She testified that she used the pillowcase to wipe her vagina?

A: I believe so.

Q: That is what she testified to on the stand yesterday, is it not?

A: Yes.

Q: If she was bleeding and wiped herself with the pillowcase, you would expect to find blood on the pillowcase?

A: Not being there when that took place, uhh, I do note that there was no staining that was indicative of blood staining identified on the pillowcase.

Q: If she was bleeding and wiped herself with the pillowcase, you would expect to find blood on the pillowcase?

A: Again, I don't know.

Q: But you do know there was no blood on the pillowcase?

A: No, there was not.

Q: There was no blood found on the sheets?

A: No blood was identified.

Q: You also tested her clothing?

A: Yes, I did.

Q: This included a skirt, the underwear, and a shirt.

A: Yes, that is correct.

Q: There was no blood found on the skirt?

A: Correct.

Q: There was no blood found on the underwear?

A: Correct.

Q: There was no blood found on the shirt?

A: Correct.

Q: There was no blood found on any clothing?

A: Correct.

Q: There was no semen found on the skirt?

A: Correct.

Q: There was no semen found on the underwear?

A: Correct.

Q: There was no semen found on the shirt?

A: Correct.

Q: There was no semen found on any clothing?

A: No semen was identified on any of the clothing.

Q: The witness testified that she put on her underwear while she was bleeding from the vagina?

A: Yes.

Q: You expect to find blood on her underwear?

A: You could possibly find blood on the underwear, however, it is not uncommon to find residual blood staining on female underwear just through, you know, menstrual cycles. Sometimes you do have blood that would be found there. So whether or not it would be of forensic importance, from my standpoint, but no blood was identified on the underwear.

Q: You expected to find blood on her underwear?

A: Like I said, no blood was found.

Q: You never expected to find blood on her underwear?

A: I thought it was a possibility.

Q: There was no blood on the underwear?

A: No, there was not.

Q: There was no menstrual blood found?

A: No.

Q: You found no blood from injuries?

A: No.

Q: There was no blood found, whatsoever?

A: No.

DNA TYPING

Point: Improperly handled DNA evidence can be contaminated.

Q: I want to talk to you about DNA typing, do you understand?

Q: DNA typing has revolutionized the analysis of biological evidence?

Q: It is now possible to obtain very discriminating information from a wide variety of biological evidence?

Q: This information allows evidence collected from the patient, suspect, or crime scene to be linked?

Q: DNA testing is now sufficiently sensitive that valuable genetic information can be routinely obtained from very small or old evidence samples?

Q: A much higher success rate is now possible for typing small evidence samples such as fingernail scrapings, vulvar, vestibular, penile/scrotum swabs, and saliva samples from areas where a victim was licked or kissed?

Q: Along with the increased sensitivity of DNA testing, however, comes a heightened concern regarding the possibility of contaminating evidence samples?

Q: It is important that anything, such as implements or gloves, used to collect or hold samples be adequately cleaned between samples?

Q: When DNA evidence is not properly handled, it can become easily contaminated?

Q: DNA evidence must be properly handled to avoid contamination?

Q: It is important to avoid contamination of any evidence?

Q: Particular care must be taken when collecting evidence for possible DNA analysis?

Q: Particular care must be taken because DNA analysis is extremely sensitive, and allows typing of very small samples?

Point: DNA evidence contamination has several causes.

Q: Contamination can happen in a number of ways?

Q: Contamination can occur from the examiner to the patient?

Q: Contamination can occur from the examination environment to the patient?

Q: Contamination can occur from one piece of evidence to another?

Point: Examiners can contaminate the patient.

Q: Let's talk about how the examiner can contaminate the patient, okay?

Q: The examiner can contaminate the patient by not wearing gloves as needed?

Q: The examiner can contaminate the patient by not changing gloves as needed?

Q: The examiner can contaminate the patient by not wearing a face mask?

Q: The examiner can contaminate the patient by coughing or sneezing on or near the patient without a mask?

Q: The examiner can contaminate the patient by touching a non-sterile surface during the examination?

Q: The examiner can contaminate the patient by shedding skin cells during the examination?

Point: The examination environment can cause contamination.

Q: Let's talk about how the examination environment can contaminate the patient, okay?

Q: The examination environment can contaminate the patient when the examination area is not thoroughly cleaned before the examination?

Q: The examination environment can contaminate the patient when the examination area is not thoroughly cleaned between examinations?

Q: The examination environment can contaminate the patient when the evidence processing area is not thoroughly cleaned before and after examinations?

Q: Examiner protocols require that the examination area be thoroughly cleaned before and after each examination?

Q: You are required to document that this step was accomplished?

Q: Examiner protocols require that the evidence processing area be thoroughly cleaned before and after each exam is processed?

Q: You are required to document that this step was accomplished?

Q: In this case, this step did not occur?

Point: Evidence can contaminate other pieces of evidence.

Q: Let's talk about how one piece of evidence can contaminate another piece of evidence, okay?

Q: One piece of evidence can contaminate another when evidence is not packaged separately?

Q: One piece of evidence can contaminate another when biological samples are not packaged separately?

Q: One piece of evidence can contaminate another during the drying process?

Q: One piece of evidence can contaminate another when samples from different patients are packaged together?

Q: You are required to package samples from different patient examinations separately?

BIOLOGICAL EVIDENCE: COLLECTION OF SAMPLES FROM THE HEAD, HAIR, AND BODY

Point: Specific procedures for collecting dried and moist secretions and stains must be followed.

Q: When collecting dried and moist secretions and stains from a patient's head, hair, scalp, and body, specific procedures must be followed?

Q: Examples of dried or moist secretions include semen, blood, and saliva from bites, suction injuries like hickeys, licking, and kissing?

Q: When the stain is moist you should swab it with a dry swab to avoid dilution?

Q: You should collect the entire stain, using several swabs?

Q: When the stain is dried, you should moisten the swab with sterile, deionized, or distilled water?

Q: The entire stain should be collected, using several moistened swabs if necessary?

Point: Procedures for collecting secretion control swabs must be followed.

Q: When collecting secretions, it is important to collect a control swab from the patient?

Q: The control swab provides the crime laboratory with "baseline" information regarding the patient's own secretions?

Q: The control swab also gives the crime laboratory "baseline" information regarding possible contaminants adjacent to the stained area?

Q: The analyst uses information developed from analysis of the control swab to interpret the results from the evidence swab?

Q: When collecting control swabs from a patient, specific procedures must be followed?

Q: The control swab should be collected by moistening a swab with sterile, deionized, or distilled water?

Q: Then, using this swab, you swab an unstained area adjacent to the stain?

Q: It is crucial that you swab an area that is unstained?

Q: For example, if the stain is on the right arm, you should collect the control swab from an unstained area near the stain on the same arm?

Q: You should collect one control swab for each stain collected, unless several stains are collected within a small area?

Q: In that case, one control swab is sufficient?

Q: Then, you should carefully label the control and evidence swabs, air dry, and package them in separate containers?

Point: Procedures for collecting matted hair must be followed.

Q: When collecting matted hair from a patient, specific procedures must be followed?

Q: You should cut matted head, facial, pubic, or body hairs bearing crusted material and place them in a bindle?

Q: These samples may consist of undiluted semen and can be a valuable source of genetic information regarding the suspect?

Q: All swabs and slides must be air dried prior to packaging?

Point: Procedures for collecting oral samples must be followed.

Q: When collecting oral samples from a patient, specific procedures must be followed?

Q: Since mixtures of semen and saliva may be present in the perioral area, you should examine this area carefully?

Q: Semen is rapidly lost from the mouth by dilution with saliva, swallowing, eating, and drinking?

Q: If less than 12 hours have passed since the incident, you should collect two oral swabs by swabbing firmly around the gums, frenulum, and in the fold of the cheeks?

CHAPTER 6: CROSS EXAMINING LAW ENFORCEMENT

PRELIMINARY STEPS AT A CRIME SCENE

Point: Procedures for investigating a crime scene.

Q: There are proper steps and procedures for investigating a crime scene?

Q: Trying to handle every crime scene in the same exact way would not be effective?

Q: In many cases, the first responding officer will have the first contact with the alleged victim and the scene?

Q: In this first approach, the officer is often concerned with personal safety?

Q: Crime scenes can be dangerous places?

Q: In a sexual assault scene, there can be biohazards like blood-borne diseases?

Q: In many cases, the suspect will not be at the scene of the assault?

Q: The officer should attempt to identify the way the suspect left the scene?

Q: The officer should take care not to disturb any evidence left by the suspect during the suspect's departure?

Q: The officer should also be alert to potential witnesses and other sources of information?

Point: Procedures for securing and protecting the scene.

Q: The first responding officer is often not sufficient to investigate the scene?

Q: The first responding officer should make sure the scene is protected from contamination and alteration until further investigators arrive?

Q: The first responding officer should make sure the scene is protected from alteration?

Q: To secure the scene, the officer should establish boundaries?

Q: In making these boundaries, the officer should avoid disturbing the evidence as much as he/she can?

Q: Any alterations to the scene that occur in the process of securing the scene should be documented?

Q: After the boundaries have been established, there should be only one entry point into the scene?

Q: This allows for control of personnel who have access to the crime scene?

Q: The name of anyone who enters and leaves the scene should be recorded?

Q: Persons who do not have legitimate activity in the crime scene should not be allowed?

Point: Procedures for conducting a preliminary survey.

Q: Once the scene is secured, the individual in charge of the investigation should conduct a preliminary survey of the scene?

Q: A preliminary survey is a brief walk through of the scene?

Q: During the preliminary survey, the officer in charge determines how big the search area is?

Q: The officer identifies personnel and equipment needs?

Q: The officer can identify evidence that can be easily moved or altered?

Q: During this time, photographs of the scene should be taken?

Q: The officers should make observations to help reconstruct what happened at the scene?

Q: Reconstructing what may have happened helps to guide evidence collection efforts?

Q: Once the preliminary survey has been completed, the officer should brief the remaining personnel about the condition of the scene?

Q: This makes sure that everyone with access to the scene is prepared and informed to do their jobs effectively?

Point: Procedures for documenting a scene.

Q: When documenting a scene, officers should attempt to make use of different forms of documentation like photography and notes?

Q: Documenting a scene in different ways requires the officer to think in different ways?

Q: When an officer creates a description of a scene through several different means, this allows for a more complete picture of the scene?

Q: One method of documenting the scene includes making a narrative description using written notes?

Q: Officers can also use video taping to make a narrative description?

Q: Narrative descriptions should supplement photographs and sketches of the scene?

Point: Procedures for photographing the scene.

Q: When an officer photographs a crime scene, it is better to err on the side of taking too many photographs than too little?

Q: Incomplete photography often results in an inadequately documented scene?

Q: Complete photography includes taking long-range, medium, and close-up views of the scene and the evidence?

Q: The photographer should keep a log to record the photographs taken?

Q: The photographer should use scales or identification cards in the photographs?

Q: Photographs of evidence should be made where the evidence is found?

Q: The evidence should be photographed from viewpoints that will allow a jury to understand where the evidence was located when it was found?

Q: Photographs should be taken in order to illustrate the sequence of events of the crime to others?

Q: Photographs should also be taken when the scene is released to establish the condition of the scene and answer claims that the scene was altered during investigation?

Q: Photography of individuals can record injuries to corroborate a story that's being investigated?

Point: Procedures for conducting a detailed search for evidence.

Q: Normally, the individual in charge of the crime scene investigation should not be looking for and collecting evidence?

Q: Instead, the individual in charge of the scene should look out for the needs of the individual specialists?

Q: In the process of collecting evidence, any event outside the normal scope of routine crime scene investigation should be documented?

Q: If a piece of evidence is accidentally picked up or moved, it should be documented?

Q: Any accidental alteration of the crime scene should be documented?

Point: Procedures for collecting, preserving, and documenting evidence.

Q: In the process of collecting evidence at a crime scene, it is best for a single person to be designated as the evidence custodian?

Q: The evidence custodian should be responsible for logging and sealing the evidence containers?

Q: Other officers should work with, and not independently of, that person?

Point: Procedures for conducting a final survey.

Q: After the evidence has been collected, the officer in charge should conduct a final walk through to make sure nothing has been left undone?

Q: Carefully conducting a final survey can uncover pieces of evidence that would otherwise go undiscovered?

Q: An inventory of all equipment should be used to make sure no equipment is left behind?

PROCEDURES FOR ENSURING EVIDENCE INTEGRITY

Point: Using appropriate evidence containers is crucial.

Q: When you collect evidence, you must package evidence so it cannot leak through the container?

Q: You must package evidence so it cannot be lost?

Q: You must package evidence so it cannot deteriorate?

Point: Proper steps in collecting sexual assault evidence must be followed.

Q: There are common parts of sexual assault evidence collection kits?

Q: First, you must place items in appropriate evidence containers?

Q: Then, you must label the evidence containers?

Q: You must seal the evidence containers?

Q: You must store evidence in a secure area?

Q: And, finally, you must maintain the chain of custody?

Point: Using bindles, envelopes, and boxes to protect evidence is crucial.

Q: Bindles and other small containers are used to protect items that can be easily lost, like crusted materials?

Q: Bindle paper is a clean sheet of paper that is folded to create an envelope?

Q: Once the evidence is collected, the bindle or envelope is sealed and secured?

Q: Bindle paper is used by forensic examiners to collect and transport evidence so it is not lost or contaminated?

Q: While many sophisticated techniques have emerged, the use of bindle paper remains a safe way to collect and transport forensic evidence?

Q: Bindle paper is used for trace evidence such as fibers?

Q: Bindle paper is used for trace evidence such as (hair, paint chips, crystallized or dust-like material such as drugs), or other tiny particles?

Q: This material is light and can be difficult to see?

Q: If not carefully collected and stored, this material can easily be lost or destroyed?

Q: Crusted materials include soil?

Q: Crusted materials include small fibers?

Q: Bindles and other small protective containers should be placed into evidence collection envelopes or boxes?

Q: Envelopes or boxes are used to protect evidence such as swabs?

Q: Envelopes or boxes are used to protect hair samples?

Q: Envelopes or boxes are used to protect foreign materials?

Point: Procedures for packing the sexual assault kit.

Q: A larger envelope or box should be used to hold the individual evidence?

Q: The larger package should include the collection envelopes?

Q: The larger package should include the small boxes?

Q: The larger package should include the slide mailers?

Q: The outside of the sexual assault evidence kit container must have a chain of custody form printed on it or securely attached?

Q: Clothing should be placed in paper bags?

Q: The paper bags should be clean?

Q: The paper bags should have never been used before?

Q: The paper bags should be free of all potential contaminates?

Point: Protocol for packing sexual assault evidence must be followed.

Q: Evidence collected during the sexual assault examination must be properly collected?

Q: Evidence collected during the sexual assault examination must be properly packaged?

Q: Swabs should be dried before packaging them?

Q: Dried swabs should be placed inside of never before used envelopes?

Q: Dried swabs should be placed inside of new boxes?

Q: Slides should be dried before packaging them?

Q: Dried slides should be placed inside of slide mailers?

Point: Procedures for packing small or loose foreign materials.

Q: Small or loose foreign materials should be placed inside of bindles?

Q: Small or loose material would include soil?

Q: Small or loose material would include paint?

Q: Small or loose material would include splinters?

Q: Small or loose material would include glass?

Q: Small or loose material would include fibers?

Q: Once secured, the bindles should then be placed in envelopes?

Point: Procedures for collecting blood and urine samples.

Q: Blood samples should be stored in gray stoppered blood collection vials?

Q: Urine samples should be sealed in tightly sealed clean plastic or glass containers?

Point: Procedures for sealing evidence containers.

Q: Evidence must be packaged in containers that are properly sealed?

Q: Proper sealing of containers ensures that contents cannot escape?

Q: Proper sealing of containers ensures that nothing can be added?

Q: Proper sealing of containers ensures that nothing can be altered?

Point: Evidence must be stored in a secure area.

Q: Once collected, evidence must be kept in a secure area?

Q: Once collected, evidence must be kept in a secure area when not directly in the possession of a person listed on the chain of custody?

Point: Chain of custody must be maintained.

Q: A chain of custody documents the handling of evidence?

Q: A chain of custody documents the transfer of evidence?

Q: A chain of custody documents the storage of evidence?

Q: The chain of custody begins when the evidence is first collected?

Q: The chain of custody may begin at the crime scene?

Q: The chain of custody may begin at the medical facility?

Q: The chain of custody continues with each transfer of the evidence to law enforcement, the crime laboratory, and others?

Q: You must keep complete documentation of the chain of custody?

Q: This ensures there has been no loss or alteration of evidence prior to trial?

Point: When transferring evidence, specific rules must be followed.

Q: When transferring evidence, specific rules must be followed?

Q: The rules in place are not optional?

Q: The rules are in place for a reason?

Q: You are required to follow the rules?

Q: When transferring evidence, the container must be securely taped?

Q: One should not lick the envelope?

Q: One should not lick any seal?

Q: That could transfer DNA to the package?

Q: The seal should be initialed?

Q: The seal should be dated?

Q: This is done by writing over the tape sealing the evidence container?

Q: This ensures that the package was not opened or tampered with?

Q: Stapling is not considered a secure seal?

Point: Transfers of evidence must be properly documented.

Q: Transfers of evidence must be documented with the following information:

Q: The name of the person transferring custody?

Q: The name of the person receiving custody?

Q: The date of transfer?

Q: The time of evidence transfer if required by the lab?

Q: Chain of custody information can be printed by hand on an evidence envelope or box?

Q: Chain of custody information can be securely attached to an evidence envelope or box?

Q: Chain of custody information can be preprinted on special envelopes, boxes and/or forms?

Point: Procedures for collecting evidence on clothing.

Q: Clothing worn at the time of the assault may contain useful evidence?

Q: You should examine the clothing for rips, tears, or other damage sustained as a result of the assault?

Q: This evidence could help prove whether a violent struggle occurred?

Q: You should examine the clothing for biological stains?

Q: You should examine the clothing for blood from the suspect?

Q: You should examine the clothing for saliva from the suspect?

Q: You should examine the clothing for semen from the suspect?

Q: You should examine the clothing for blood from the patient?

Q: You should examine the clothing for saliva from the patient?

Q: You should examine the clothing for semen from the patient?

Q: You should examine the clothing for pubic, head, facial or body hair foreign to the patient?

Q: You should examine the clothing for foreign materials?

Q: You should examine the clothing for fibers?

Q: You should examine the clothing for grass?

Q: You should examine the clothing for soil?

Q: You should examine the clothing for other debris from the suspect or the crime scene?

Point: Clothing worn after the assault may also hold valuable evidence.

Q: Clothing worn after the assault may also hold valuable evidence?

Q: Semen may drain from the vagina onto the underwear?

Q: The suspect's DNA may transfer onto clothing?

Q: Hairs and foreign materials may transfer from the patient's body to the clothing?

Q: You should examine the clothing worn after the assault?

Point: Procedures for collection and packaging of clothing.

Q: When collecting clothing, you must follow strict procedures?

Q: By following strict procedures, you reduce the risk of contaminating the evidence?

Q: When collecting clothing, you should have the patient remove their shoes first?

Q: Then, they disrobe on two sheets of paper placed on top of one another on the floor?

Q: The purpose of the bottom sheet is to protect the top sheet from dirt and debris on the floor?

Q: The purpose of the top sheet is to collect loose trace evidence, which may fall from the clothing during disrobing?

Q: Disposable paper used on examination tables is acceptable for this purpose?

Point: Procedures for collecting hairs, fibers, and debris.

Q: You should collect hairs, fibers, and debris on the top sheet of paper placed on the floor?

Q: After the clothing has been collected, you should fold the top sheet of paper (from the two sheets on the floor) into a large bindle?

Q: This ensures that all foreign materials are contained inside?

Q: Then you must label and seal the bindle to ensure the contents cannot escape?

Q: This bindle should then be placed into a large paper bag?

Q: The bottom sheet of paper should be discarded?

Point: Procedures for collecting semen.

Q: When collecting seminal fluid, you should focus on items that are close to the genitals?

Q: For example, underwear of the suspect?

Q: You should also focus on items that have the highest potential to contain seminal fluid according to the assault history?

Q: For example, the bed sheets, if sex occurred on the bed?

Q: As another example, if ejaculation occurred on the patient's chest, semen may be found on a shirt worn during or immediately after the assault?

Q: According to your policy, these items should be collected and placed in the evidence kit?

Point: Procedures for collecting and folding garments.

Q: When collecting and folding garments, such as a shirt, you should fold each garment as it is removed?

Q: By folding each garment separately, you prevent body fluid stains from being lost or transferred from one garment to another?

Q: By folding each garment separately, you prevent foreign materials from being lost or transferred from one garment to another?

Q: You should not fold clothing across possible body fluid stains?

Q: Doing so could transfer the body fluid stain to another garment where it did not originally exist?

Point: Procedures for collecting wet clothing.

Q: When collecting wet clothing, you must follow specific collection procedures?

Q: When collecting wet clothing, you must dry the clothing before packaging?

Q: If drying is not possible, wet clothing can be folded sandwiched between sheets of paper?

Q: After placing the item in a paper bag, you must clearly label the bag as containing a wet item?

Q: Then you must notify the law enforcement officer in charge of the case?

Q: You should immediately contact the crime laboratory to inform them there are wet items in the container?

Point: Procedures for packing clothing.

Q: When collecting clothing, specific procedures must be followed?

Q: Each item of clothing must be in an individual paper bag?

Q: You should not use plastic bags?

Q: You should not use plastic bags because plastic retains moisture?

Q: Moisture can result in mold and deterioration of biological evidence?

Q: Each clothing bag must be securely sealed?

Q: Each clothing bag must be labeled?

Q: The label should state the full name of the patient?

Q: The date of collection?

Q: The label should give a brief description of item inside?

Q: The label should have a signature or initials of the person who collected the evidence and placed it in the container?

Point: Procedures for collecting smaller items.

Q: There is a collection procedure for smaller items?

Q: You should place small bags of clothing into a larger paper bag?

Q: You should place the paper bindle from the floor into a large paper bag?

Q: You should place all bags and the bindle from the floor into a large paper bag?

Q: The large paper bag must have a chain of custody form printed on it or firmly attached?

Q: You should never put wet evidence into a bag with dry evidence?

Q: You should never put wet evidence into a bag with other wet evidence?

Q: You should let wet items dry before packing them?

Q: If this is impossible, then you should package wet evidence by itself?

Q: Otherwise, wet evidence can damage other evidence that was collected?

Q: Wet evidence can destroy other evidence that was collected?

Q: Wet evidence can contaminate other evidence that was collected?

Q: If there are multiple small containers, then you can use multiple large bags as necessary?

WOOD'S LAMP AND OR ALTERNATIVE LIGHT SOURCES

Point: Alternative light sources can find hard to see evidence.

Q: As an investigator, you can use alternative light sources to help discover evidence?

Q: The Wood's Lamp is a type of alternative light source?

Q: Basically, an alternative light source is a light?

Q: These lights have different wavelengths?

Q: You can rotate through wavelengths when looking for evidence?

Q: At certain wavelengths, evidence becomes visible?

Q: Otherwise, the evidence may not be visible to the naked eye?

Q: These lights are used to scan the body for evidence?

Q: These lights are used to scan the body for evidence such as dried or moist secretions?

Q: These lights are used to scan the body for evidence such as fluorescent fibers not readily visible in room light?

Q: These lights are used to scan the body for subtle injuries?

Q: These lights can highlight things such as semen?

Q: These lights can highlight things such as saliva?

Q: These lights can highlight things such as urine?

Q: These lights can highlight fibers?

Q: For example, carpet fibers?

Q: These lights can highlight dust or powder?

Q: These lights can highlight powder?

Q: These lights can highlight blood?

Q: These lights can highlight rope marks?

Q: These lights can highlight bite marks?

Q: These lights can highlight recent contusions?

Q: These lights can highlight other subtle injuries?

Point: Procedures when using an alternative light source.

Q: When using an alternative light source, you must follow specific procedures?

Q: Alternative light sources should be used in a darkened room?

Q: You should use the ultraviolet light to examine a patient's entire body?

Q: You should specifically examine key areas of the body?

Q: You should examine the head?

Q: You should examine the face?

Q: You should examine the hair?

Q: You should examine the lips?

Q: You should examine the mouth area?

Q: You should examine the nostrils?

Q: You should examine the neck?

Q: You should examine the chest and breasts?

Q: You should examine the external genitalia?

Q: You should examine the anal area?

Q: You should examine the inner thighs?

Q: You should examine the pubic hair?

Q: You should examine the buttocks?

Q: You should examine the anal folds?

Q: You should examine any other area indicated by the patient's history?

DETECTING SEMEN WITH AN ALTERNATIVE LIGHT SOURCE

Point: Common characteristics for detecting semen.

Q: Dried semen stains have a characteristic shiny appearance?

Q: Dried semen stains tend to flake off the skin?

Q: Semen may exhibit an off-white fluorescence under ultraviolet light?

Q: Fluorescent areas may appear as smears?

Q: Fluorescent areas may appear as streaks?

Q: Fluorescent areas may appear as splash marks?

Q: Moist semen may not fluoresce?

Q: Freshly dried semen may not fluoresce?

Point: Procedures for collecting semen.

Q: When collecting semen, specific procedures must be followed?

Q: You must swab each suspicious area?

Q: You must swab each suspicious area whether detected visually or indicated by the patient's history?

Q: You must swab each suspicious area whether it fluoresces or not?

Q: You must swab each area with separate swabs?

Q: The swabs must be moistened with sterile, deionized, or distilled water?

Q: You should collect the entire stain using several swabs, if necessary?

Q: You must then collect control swabs?

Q: You should then label and package the evidence and control swabs in separate packages?

Q: The appearance of fluorescent areas does not confirm the presence of semen?

Q: Other substances such as urine or body lotions may also fluoresce?

Q: Independent confirmation of these findings by the crime laboratory is required?

DETECTING INJURIES WITH AN ALTERNATIVE LIGHT SOURCE

Point: Alternative light sources aid in detecting subtle injuries to the head, hair, and body.

Q: Rope marks may be more visible with the aid of the Wood's Lamp or other alternate light source?

Q: Bite marks may be more visible with the aid of the Wood's Lamp or other alternate light source?

Q: Recent contusions may be more visible with the aid of the Wood's Lamp or other alternate light source?

Q: Other subtle injuries may be more visible with the aid of the Wood's Lamp or other alternate light source?

COLLECTION OF FOREIGN MATERIALS

Point: Properly collecting, comparing, and analyzing foreign materials is crucial.

Q: It is important to collect and compare foreign materials present during a sexual assault examination?

Q: Examples of foreign materials are: fibers, soil, hairs, sand, paint, glass, grass or other vegetation?

Q: Foreign materials collected from the patient's body, fingernails, and clothing can be compared to similar evidence collected from the suspect or crime scene?

Q: Pubic, head, facial, or body hair collected from the patient's body and/or clothing can be compared to reference hairs obtained from the patient?

Q: Hairs found to be foreign to the patient can then be compared to reference hairs obtained from potential suspects?

Q: Analysis of foreign materials may help establish a connection between the patient and the assailant and/or the crime scene?

Q: Analysis of foreign materials may provide information regarding the circumstances of the assault?

Q: Analysis of foreign materials may provide other valuable investigative information?

COLLECTING FINGERNAIL SCRAPINGS

Point: Collecting fingernail scrapings.

Q: I want to talk to you about the proper procedure for collecting fingernail scrapings, okay?

Q: There are two ways to collect fingernail scrapings?

Q: The first method is to use clean toothpicks or manicure sticks to collect scrapings from under the fingernails?

Q: You then place scrapings from each hand into separate containers?

Q: The second method is to use clean fingernail cutters or scissors to cut the fingernails?

Q: You then place cuttings from each hand into separate containers or bindles?

COLLECTING SMALL FOREIGN MATERIALS SUCH AS FIBERS, PAINT, SPLINTERS, GLASS

Point: Collecting small or loose foreign materials.

Q: I want to talk to you about the proper procedure for collecting small or loose foreign materials, okay?

Q: Small or loose foreign materials include fibers, paint, splinters, and glass?

Q: One option is to remove the material with forceps?

Q: You could also gently scrape the materials with a clean slide or back of a scalpel blade?

Q: In the case of fiber evidence, you would collect it with transparent tape?

Q: You would use the sticky side of a piece of transparent tape to remove the materials from the surface?

Q: You then place the tape sticky side down onto a transparent material, such as a Ziplock plastic bag turned inside out?

Q: Then, you turn the bag right side out and seal it?

COLLECTING PUBIC HAIR COMBINGS OR BRUSHINGS

Point: Collecting pubic hair combings or brushings.

Q: I want to talk to you about the proper procedure for collecting pubic hair combings or brushings, do you understand?

Q: To collect pubic hair combings or brushings, you place a paper sheet under the patient's buttocks?

Q: You then comb the pubic hair downward to remove loose hairs and/or foreign materials?

Q: You then fold the paper into a bindle with the comb or brush inside?

Q: You then place bindles and other small protective containers into the evidence collection envelopes?

COLLECTING BIOLOGICAL EVIDENCE

Point: Collecting biological evidence.

Q: I want to talk to you about the proper procedures for collecting biological evidence, okay?

Q: Biological evidence should be collected based on the visual and Wood's Lamp examination?

Q: Biological evidence can also be collected based on the patient's history?

Q: Patient history may lead the medical examiner to biological evidence that is not otherwise visible?

Q: Biological evidence includes samples such as semen?

Q: Blood?

Q: Vaginal secretions?

Q: Vaginal epithelial cells recovered from the suspect's genitals or from condoms?

Q: Saliva?

Q: Saliva can be left from bites?

Q: Saliva can be left from hickeys?

Q: Saliva can be left from licking?

Q: Saliva can be left from kissing?

Q: Saliva can be left from oral sex?

Q: The crime laboratory can examine multiple items for biological evidence?

Q: The lab can examine a patient's clothing?

Q: The lab can examine swabs of dried and moist stains from the patient's body, head, and hair?

Q: The lab can examine vulvar, vestibular, vaginal, cervical, oral, anal, and/or rectal swabs and slides?

Q: The lab can examine cuttings of matted hair?

Q: The lab can examine pubic hair combings?

Q: The lab can examine fingernail scrapings?

Q: The lab can examine swabs of the suspect's genitalia?

Q: Body fluid present in these samples can be identified and genetically typed by the crime laboratory?

Q: The information derived from the analysis can be helpful in an investigation?

Q: It can be used to determine whether sexual contact occurred?

Q: It can be used to provide information regarding the circumstances of the incident?

Q: It can be compared to reference samples collected from victims and suspected assailants?

INVESTIGATIVE BIAS

Most criminal investigators believe that they are fair, neutral, and unbiased. The reality is, most are biased in favor of the alleged victim, although few will admit it.

Many investigators believe that a victim would never lie and they assume everything the victim says is true. When this happens, investigators become blinded by their bias and only look for facts that support the victim's story and prove the guilt of the suspect, often overlooking exculpatory evidence. The cross examiner must expose investigative bias in front of the jury.

Point: The investigator does not know the alleged victim.

Q: Investigator _____, when this investigation started, you had never met the victim?

Q: She told you a story about what happened?

Q: You did not know anything about her background?

Q: You did not know anything about her history?

Q: You did not know whether she had psychological issues?

Q: You did not know whether she was a known liar?

Q: You did not know whether she was a known exaggerator?

Q: You did not know whether she was a drama queen?

Q: You did not know whether she had a reputation for being truthful?

Q: You did not know whether she had lied in the past?

Q: You did not know whether she had lied in the past, about anything whatsoever?

Point: The investigator does not know the accused.

Q: When this investigation started, you had never met the accused?

Q: You did not know anything about his background?

Q: You did not know anything about his history?

Q: You did not know whether he was a known liar?

Q: You did not know whether he was a known exaggerator?

Q: You did not know whether he was a drama queen?

Q: You did not know whether he had a reputation for being truthful?

Q: You did not know whether he had lied in the past?

Point: The investigator investigated the accused.

Q: After the report was made, you began to investigate the accused?

Q: You called some of his friends?

Q: You called some of his coworkers?

Q: You called some of his past girlfriends?

Q: You called some of his ex-wives?

Q: You called some of his neighbors?

Q: You called some of his classmates?

Q: You called some of his employers?

Q: You called some of his family members?

Q: You called witnesses who knew him?

Q: You did this to learn more information about him?

Q: You did this to learn who he was?

Q: You did this to learn what type of person he is?

Q: You did this to learn his reputation in the community?

Q: You did this to determine whether he has a pattern of misconduct?

Q: You wanted to see if he is a liar?

Q: You wanted to see if he is an exaggerator?

Q: You wanted to see if he is truthful?

Q: You interviewed witnesses to see if he changed his story?

Q: You wanted to catch him in a lie?

Point: The investigator did not investigate the alleged victim.

Q: You said you have to remain impartial?

Q: What does that mean, impartial?

Q: Your training requires you to remain impartial?

Q: You said you have to remain unbiased?

Q: What does that mean, unbiased?

Q: Your training requires you to remain unbiased?

Q: You said you have to investigate all leads?

Q: That would include the person making the allegation?

Q: She is, after all, the key evidence in this case?

Q: Her testimony is key evidence in this case?

Q: Her credibility is a key issue in this case?

Q: You have already testified you did not know anything about the alleged victim when this case started?

Q: You would agree that if she is a known liar, that could be important in this case?

Q: You would agree that if she has a history of lying, that could be important in this case?

Q: You would agree that if she has a psychiatric history, that could be important in this case?

Q: You would agree that if she is a known exaggerator, that could be important in this case?

Q: You would agree that if she has made false reports in the past, that could be important in this case?

Q: You knew nothing about the accused when the case started?

Q: So you investigated the background of the accused?

Q: Let's talk about what steps you took to learn more about the person reporting a crime?

Q: After the report was made, did you investigate the alleged victim?

Q: You didn't ask her friends what type of person she is?

Q: You didn't ask her coworkers what type of person she is?

Q: You didn't ask her past boyfriends what type of person she is?

Q: You didn't ask her ex-husband(s) what type of person she is?

Q: You didn't ask her neighbors what type of person she is?

Q: You didn't ask her classmates what type of person she is?

Q: You didn't ask her employer(s) what type of person she is?

Q: You didn't ask her family members what type of person she is?

Q: You did not interview anyone in order to learn more information about her?

Q: You did not interview the people we just mentioned to determine whether she has a pattern of misconduct?

Q: You did not interview these people to determine whether she is untruthful?

Q: You did not interview these people to determine whether she is an exaggerator?

Q: You did not interview these people to determine whether she is a known liar?

Q: You did not interview these people to see if she changed her story?

Q: You did not try to catch her in a lie?

Q: Your training requires you to remain impartial?

Q: Your training requires you to remain unbiased?

Q: Your job requires you to remain impartial?

Q: Your job requires you to remain unbiased?

Q: When you are not impartial, mistakes can be made?

Point: An investigator should not jump to conclusions.

Q: At the academy, you were taught you should not jump to conclusions?

Q: Your training manuals taught you to not jump to conclusions?

Q: As an investigator, when you jump to conclusions, you may overlook key facts?

Q: As an investigator, when you jump to conclusions, you may overlook key evidence?

Q: As an investigator, when you jump to conclusions, you may overlook key witnesses?

Q: That is why, as an investigator, you must follow up on all relevant leads?

Q: That is why, as an investigator, you must follow up on all relevant evidence?

Q: If you jump to conclusions, an innocent person may go to jail?

Q: If you jump to conclusions, a guilty person may go free?

Q: If you don't follow up on all relevant leads, a guilty person may go free?

Q: If you don't follow up on all relevant leads, an innocent person may go to jail?

Point: An investigator should not contaminate witness testimony.

....

Q: As a special agent, you must remain neutral?

Q: As a special agent, you must remain detached?

Q: As a special agent, you must remain impartial?

Q: You are a neutral fact finder?

Q: Your job is not to take sides, right?

Q: Your job is to collect evidence?

Q: And present the evidence to the prosecution?

Q: In this trial, we're here to decide whether or not a sexual assault occurred?

Q: The jury must decide whether or not the sex was consensual?

Q: That's not your job to say whether it was or was not, is it?

Q: It is not your job to jump to a conclusion about what happened in the case?

Q: One of the most important things in your job is to follow up with leads in the case?

Q: A witness is a potential lead?

Q: One of the most important things in your job is to interview relevant witnesses?

Q: You're trained to document and take statements from witnesses?

Q: Witnesses should be interviewed in a timely manner?

Q: As quickly as possible?

Q: This is what they teach you in your training?

Q: This is what it states in your training manuals?

Q: You should interview witnesses while their memory is fresh?

Q: You should interview witnesses while their memory is clear?

Q: You should interview witnesses while their memory is uncontaminated?

Q: In other words, before they start talking to other witnesses about what happened?

Q: Here, the witnesses were not interviewed until weeks later?

Point: Lead investigator is responsible for overseeing the investigation and case file.

Q: Special Agent, before you came here to testify, did you not review the case file?

Q: You were the lead case agent in this case?

Q: You were responsible for overseeing the investigation?

Q: As the lead case agent, you compiled a case file?

Q: The case file details every investigative step taken in this case?

Q: It lists who was interviewed?

Q: When they were interviewed?

Q: Where they were interviewed?

Q: And who did the interview?

Q: The report also has a summary of what each witness said?

Q: The report also contains the sworn statement made by the witnesses?

Q: The report also contains a document on which the witness swears under oath that the statement is true?

Q: All of that information is contained in the report of investigation?

Q: The report of investigation that you compiled?

Q: The report of investigation that you reviewed as this case progressed?

Q: You were the first responder in this case?

Q: A first responder is the first member of law enforcement to arrive on the scene?

Q: As a first responder, one of your primary duties is to secure the crime scene?

Q: As a first responder, one of your primary duties is to preserve evidence at the scene?

Q: As a first responder, one of your primary duties is to conduct initial interviews?

DEALING WITH AN AGENT WHO HAS "MEMORY LOSS"

For defense lawyers, one of the most terrifying aspects of a jury trial is cross examining investigators. Investigators are usually helpful and well prepared when testifying for the government. However, when they are cross examined by the defense, they become evasive, non-responsive, or simply get amnesia. They are trained to answer questions this way. After all, they want the defendant in jail.

Point: Investigator has selective amnesia.

Q: You were the lead case agent in this case?

A: Yes.

Q: Being the lead case agent is an important job?

A: Yes.

Q: To be the lead case agent is a great responsibility?

A: Yes.

Q: You must pay attention to details and facts?

A: I do.

Q: Your job is to collect evidence?

A: It is.

Q: To document evidence?

A: Yes.

Q: All relevant evidence?

A: Yes.

Q: Not just evidence that helps the prosecution?

A: Correct.

Q: Your job is to find the truth?

A: Yes.

Q: That is what you did in this case?

A: Yes, I did.

Q: As the lead case agent, you were aware that the alleged victim claimed to have been raped?

A: Yes, violently.

Q: Violently raped?

A: Yes.

Q: Anally raped?

A: Yes.

Q: Vaginally raped?

A: Yes.

Q: With violent force?

A: Yes.

Q: You went to the dorm room to investigate?

A: Yes, I did.

Q: You brought a camera?

A: Yes.

Q: That was to document what you found?

A: Correct.

Q: You brought another CID agent as backup?

A: Yes, I did.

Q: You did this to help with collecting and processing evidence?

A: Yes.

Q: At the crime scene, you were the boss?

A: Yes.

Q: You were the lead case agent?

A: Yes.

Q: You went to the dorm room to look at the bed?

A: Yes.

Q: The bed where the crime happened?

A: Correct.

Q: To collect evidence from the bed?

A: Yes.

Q: The sheets?

A: Yes.

Q: The pillow cases?

A: Yes.

Q: The comforter?

A: Yes.

Q: The towel from the bathroom?

A: Yes.

Q: You went to look for blood?

A: Yes, I did.

Q: You looked for blood on the sheets?

A: I did.

Q: On the pillow case?

A: Yes.

Q: On the towel?

A: Yes.

Q: You did this to prove or disprove if a rape happened?

A: I did it to collect all relevant evidence.

Q: Right, you did it to collect evidence?

A: Yes.

Q: Evidence to help determine if a rape happened?

A: Yes.

Q: Special Agent, you collected the white sheet from the bed?

A: Yes, I did.

Q: You collected the white sheet from the bed where the alleged victim claims she was raped?

A: Yes.

Q: The sheet was still on the bed when you took it?

A: I don't remember.

Q: You do not remember where the sheet was located when you first entered the dorm room?

A: No, I don't recall. It has been over 10 months.

Q: If I show you your investigative report, would that refresh your memory?

A: I guess it would.

(*Mark the report as a Defense Exhibit for identification and show it to the witness.*)

Q: Please direct your attention to page 3 of the report. Please look at the last paragraph and read it. When you are finished reading it, please look up at me.

A: Okay.

Q: Does that refresh your memory about the location of the sheet when you entered the room?

A: Yes.

Q: The white sheet was on the bed when you entered the dorm room?

A: Yes, according to this report.

Q: You seized that sheet?

A: That is what the report says.

Q: You wrote the report?

A: Yes.

Q: You paid close attention to detail when you wrote the report?

A: Yes.

Q: Your report accurately describes what you saw and what you did?

A: Yes.

Q: You seized the sheet that was on the bed?

A: According to the report.

Q: Is your report accurate?

A: Yes.

Q: Is your report the truth?

A: Yes.

Scolding the Agent

An alternate way to approach this witness would be the following:

Q: You took the white sheet that was on the bed?

A: According to the report.

Q: Special Agent John Smith, I am not asking what the report says; I am asking you what you did. Do you understand the difference?

A: Yes, sir.

Q: You, Special Agent Smith, removed the sheet from the bed?

A: Yes.

Embarrassing the Agent

For this scenario, you are in jury trial, and the special agent is testifying during cross examination. The agent claims to not remember key facts, and the defense lawyer must keep refreshing his memory. It is bogging down the cross examination. It is now time to embarrass the special agent and prove he is lazy, biased, and incompetent.

Q: Special Agent Smith, you were the lead case agent in this case?

A: Yes.

Q: Being the lead case agent is an important job?

A: Yes.

Q: To be the lead case agent is a great responsibility?

A: Yes.

Q: You must pay attention to details and facts?

A: Yes, I do.

Q: You seem to have forgotten a lot of the facts of this case, however. Would you agree?

A: Well, it has been 10 months.

Q: Whether it has been 10 months or 10 years, your job is to testify accurately to the facts?

A: Yeah.

Q: You have had 10 months to review the case file?

A: Yes.

Q: You have had the case file in your possession for 10 months?

A: Yes, I have.

Q: You wrote most of the words contained in that file?

A: Yes, I did.

Q: You then reviewed the details of the case file for accuracy?

A: Correct.

Q: You have met with the prosecution numerous times regarding this case?

A: Yes.

Q: You testified two months ago at the preliminary hearing?

A: Yes.

Q: You were aware this case was going to trial for a long time?

A: Yes.

Q: You knew you were testifying in this trial?

A: Yes.

Q: You have known that for several months?

A: Blah, blah.

Q: You chose to not review your case file during that time?

A: Blah, blah.

Q: You chose to not review your case file before taking the stand?

A: Blah, blah.

Q: You made that decision, knowing how serious the charges were in this case?

A: Blah, blah.

Q: You made that decision, knowing the accused faces 80 years in prison?

A: Blah, blah.

Q: You made the decision to not review the file, knowing your testimony would be vital in this case?

A: Blah, blah.

Q: Two weeks ago, you received notification that you would have to come here today and testify to the facts of this case?

A: Correct.

Q: Again, you chose to not review your case file after you were ordered to come and testify?

A: Blah, blah.

Q: This trial started on Monday?

A: Correct.

Q: Today is Wednesday?

A: Yes.

Q: You have been sitting in the witness waiting room for two days?

A: Yes.

Q: The witness waiting room is across the hallway, outside of the court room?

A: Yes.

Q: You have been sitting in that room with the case file in your possession?

A: I have.

Q: For two days?

A: Yes.

Q: You have been reading magazines?

A: Sometimes.

Q: Watching TV?

A: A little.

Q: You have been sitting there talking to other witnesses?

A: Not much.

Q: Joking around?

A: Some.

Q: While sitting there, knowing that your testimony was eminent, you chose to not look at your case file?

A: Yes.

Q: That was a conscious decision that you made?

A: I don't recall.

Q: Your training taught you to review the case file before testifying?

A: Yes.

Q: Your field manual taught you to review the case file before testifying?

A: Yes.

Q: That is so your testimony is accurate?

A: Yes.

Q: That makes sense, right... to be prepared before testifying in a serious case?

A: Yes.

Q: Now, do you need time to review your case file before we proceed?

At this point, the agent has been embarrassed. But, he deserved it. If done at the right time and in the right professional tone, the jury will not hold it against you for scolding the investigator.

This technique should only be used on investigators who repeatedly feign amnesia. Do not use this scolding technique when the witness remembers most of the facts but needs help on specific detail-oriented facts, such as phone numbers, addresses, inventories, and other details that no human could recite from memory. If you attack an agent because he cannot recite intricate details then you look foolish, and you lose credibility. Attacking investigators over trivial matters usually backfires.

FALSE ACCUSATIONS

Point: False allegations happen (introductory questions).

Q: False allegations can happen in criminal cases?

Q: False allegations can happen in rape/sexual assault cases?

Q: A victim repeatedly changing his or her account of the assault may indicate a false allegation?

Q: Investigators should be careful to distinguish a true changing of the story from a real recollection of additional information?

Q: In both true and false claims, new information and details may be added in later interviews?

Q: In false allegations, the claimant can try to "shore up" the allegation to make it more believable?

Q: Investigators should be careful to distinguish between deliberate deceit and an honest mistake?

Q: In the early stages of an investigation, a legitimate rape victim may provide incorrect information because of stress or mental trauma?

Q: This trauma and stress leads to an altered ability to process information?

Q: In a false allegation, the person making the allegation may offer information that's different from the original report?

Q: This is to further deceive and mislead the investigators?

Q: Investigators should be sensitive to the possibility of a false report?

TIMING OF FALSE ALLEGATIONS

Point: False allegations are typically reported with 24 hours of the incident.

Q: You are familiar with medical literature on sexual assault?

Q: You are familiar with law enforcement literature on sexual assault?

Q: When I say literature, I am talking about textbooks and articles written by experts, do you understand?

Q: This literature discusses the reporting of sexual assaults?

Q: The FBI keeps statistics on sexual assault reporting?

Q: According to this literature, false allegations are typically reported with 24 hours of the incident?

INVESTIGATORS SHOULD CONSIDER FALSE ALLEGATION AS A POSSIBILITY

Point: False allegation of sexual assault should be considered.

Q: As an investigator, false allegation may be considered when the findings are inconsistent with the report made?

Q: As an investigator, false allegation may be considered when the evidence is inconsistent with the report made?

Q: For example, if a victim reports they were beaten, choked, and thrown in the dirt several hours prior, and you see no evidence that would corroborate the story, then a false allegation may be considered?

A: It doesn't mean she is not telling the truth.

Q: It also does not mean she *is* telling the truth?

Q: As an investigator, you have a duty to investigate?

Q: You have a duty to follow up on her story?

Q: You have a duty to interview *all* relevant witnesses?

Q: You have a duty to collect evidence?

Q: You have a duty to preserve evidence?

Q: You have a duty to investigate whether a crime occurred?

Q: You have a duty to determine whether she is telling the truth?

Q: As an investigator, you don't just take someone's word at face value?

Q: As an investigator, your job does not end once an allegation is made?

Q: As an investigator, your job is just beginning when the report is made?

Q: As an investigator, your job is to remain impartial?

Q: As an investigator, your job is to remain unbiased?

Q: As an investigator, your job is to remain impartial?

Q: As an investigator, you do not take sides?

Q: As an investigator, your job is to investigate?

Point: A sex-stress situation can lead to a false accusation.

Q: One situation that can produce a false rape allegation is called a "sex-stress" situation?

Q: Sex-stress situations are cases where two partners first agree to have sexual contact?

Q: Then, something "goes wrong?"

Q: Often, the problem can involve a third party, such as a friend, a boyfriend, or husband?

Q: The third party may become aware of the sexual contact?

Q: The third party may define the sexual contact as a rape?

Q: The third party may convince one of the partners to the sexual contact to say it was a rape?

Q: One of the partners to the sexual contact may say it was a rape as a way out of a dilemma with the third party?

Q: There are different types of sex-stress situations?

Q: One type of sex-stress situation involves mutual agreement?

Q: In mutual agreement cases, both partners agree to have sex but then one partner wishes to deny the act?

Q: Another kind of sex-stress situation involving mutual agreement can be where both partners agree to have sex and one partner does things that makes the other uncomfortable?

Q: In another kind of sex-stress situation, the parents of one partner may become involved?

Q: The parents may perceive that sex has occurred?

Q: The parents may perceive that their son/daughter's reputation may be endangered?

Q: The daughter may describe the sex as rape to the parents to receive pregnancy prevention advice?

Q: One type of sex-stress situation involves financial gain?

Q: Sometimes, sex workers can have customers who do not pay what they agreed?

Q: Sometimes, clients don't pay the sex worker at all?

Q: Sometimes, clients rob the sex worker?

Q: It is becoming more common for sex workers to turn to police for help?

Point: Most false victims are motivated by the need to avoid unwanted consequences.

Q: Often, the false victim is motivated by the need to avoid unwanted consequences?

Q: The false victim can be motivated by the need to cover up for inappropriate behavior?

Q: The false victim can have a financial motive?

Point: Delusional people sometimes make false rape allegations.

Q: A false rape allegation can also come from complainants who are psychotic or delusional?

Q: In some cases, the false victim may make several different complaints?

Point: Overview of people who make false allegations.

Q: Generally, people who make false rape allegations tend to be female?

Q: People who make false rape allegations tend to be white/Caucasian?

Q: People who make false rape allegations tend to be between 21 and 30 years old?

Q: False complaints can be made by people with any level of education?

Q: False complaints can be made by people of any profession?

Q: False complaints can be made by people of any intellectual capability?

REASONS FOR FALSE ALLEGATIONS

Point: There are various reasons why false allegations are made.

Q: People who make false allegations may have legitimate problems that are worthy of attention?

Q: If the allegation is accepted at face value instead of being investigated, those problems may go untreated?

Q: They can also result in future false reports?

Q: People can make false complaints for a number of different reasons?

Point: Some false allegations are made to get attention/ sympathy.

Q: Some people make false complaints to get attention or sympathy?

Q: They may want attention or sympathy from friends?

Q: They may want attention or sympathy from relatives?

Q: They may want attention or sympathy from the authorities?

Q: These people usually have strong feelings of inadequacy?

Q: These people crave concern or support or attention?

Q: These people may have tried other methods of getting attention, like faking an illness?

Q: For people in need of attention, the support they get from others after a false complaint may fulfill their needs?

Q: But in typical rape situations, even very strong demonstrations of support can't fully alleviate what the victim feels?

Point: Some false allegations of sexual assault are made to conceal adultery.

Q: For example, a false allegation may be motivated by the need to conceal consensual sexual intercourse?

Q: When a spouse is caught cheating, they may want to cover it up?

Q: They will claim they were assaulted, rather than admitting they cheated?

Q: That's one common example, according to your training, where a false allegation is made?

Q: Another example is if a woman cheats on her boyfriend and she does not want to get caught?

Q: They will claim they were assaulted, rather than admitting they cheated?

Q: That's another example, according to your training, where a false allegation is made?

Q: You were taught that false allegations of sexual assault are sometimes made to conceal adultery?

Point: Some false allegations of sexual assault are made to explain an STD.

Q: False allegations of sexual assault may be motivated by the need for antibiotics to treat potential STDs?

Q: False allegations of sexual assault may be made to cover up an STD?

Q: For example, when a spouse commits adultery and contracts an STD, they may not want to admit they cheated?

Q: Claiming the STD came from a sexual assault is one motivation to make a false allegation?

Q: You were taught that false allegations of sexual assault are sometimes made to explain an STD?

Point: Some false allegations of sexual assault are made to explain a pregnancy.

Q: False allegations of sexual assault may be motivated by the need to explain a pregnancy?

Q: You were taught that some false allegations of sexual assault are motivated by the need to explain a pregnancy?

Point: Some false allegations of sexual assault may be motivated by regret or shame.

Q: False allegations of sexual assault may be motivated by regret or shame?

Q: You were taught that some false allegations of sexual assault are motivated by regret or shame?

Point: Some false allegations of sexual assault may be motivated by the need to create an alibi.

Q: Some false allegations are made to create an alibi?

Q: Some people make false complaints to avoid unwanted consequences?

Q: One example of unwanted consequences may be a teenage girl alleging rape if she stays out overnight without her parent's permission and gets caught?

Q: Some people make false complaints to cover up for inappropriate behavior?

Q: A person may make a rape allegation to cover up infidelity or cheating?

Q: An alibi is an excuse or defense?

Q: If a woman is caught having sex by her boyfriend, claiming she didn't want it could be an alibi?

Q: Claiming she had too much to drink could be an alibi?

Q: Claiming she did not remember what happened could be an alibi?

Q: You were taught that some false allegations of sexual assault are motivated by the need to create an alibi?

Point: Some false allegations are made due to anger or revenge.

Q: Some people make false complaints out of anger?

Q: Some people make false complaints for revenge?

Q: These people were usually emotionally involved with the person they name as the perpetrator?

Q: These people are motivated by a desire to get even with the person they name as the perpetrator for real or imagined wrongs?

Q: Because these false complaints identify the alleged perpetrator, these can pose a great danger to the person targeted?

Q: In these situations, it is common for the false victim to withdraw the complaint after the investigation is initiated?

Q: In these situations, it is common for the false victim to modify the complaint after the investigation is initiated?

Point: There are factors consistent with false allegations.

Q: Legitimate rape reports may involve some level of misperception of the assault?

Q: Because of the potential for misperception, it is important that every aspect of the report be scrutinized?

Q: There are several features that can indicate the complainant has misperceived the events of the assault?

Q: These features can also be consistent with a false allegation?

Point: The manner in which a rape is reported can be significant.

Q: The manner in which a rape allegation is reported can be significant?

Q: In both legitimate and false rape complaints, there are often delays in making a report?

Q: The report is often made to someone other than the police?

Q: In false reports, the false victim may attempt to direct the discussion to safe areas?

Q: Safe areas include discussions of force?

Q: Safe areas include discussions of injuries?

Q: Safe areas include discussions of resistance?

Q: On the other hand, the false victim may avoid discussing facts about the assault itself or the offender?

Q: The initial report may be extremely vague?

Q: The initial report may be unnecessarily detailed?

Q: Typically, false victims report a large and overpowering offender?

Q: False victims may report multiple offenders?

Q: False victims may be vague about their connection to the offender if there is any connection?

Q: False victims typically report only those sexual acts in which they normally engage in?

Q: For example, a person who does not engage in anal sex is unlikely to falsely report anal rape?

Point: The absence of evidence usually associated with rape can indicate a false allegation.

Q: An absence of evidence usually associated with rape can indicate a false allegation of rape?

Q: In false allegations, the reported crime scene may not support the complainant's report?

Q: Damage to clothing may be inconsistent with the location of injuries in false allegations?

Point: A false victim usually has no injuries or superficial injuries.

Q: It is uncommon for persons who make false claims to show injuries?

Q: When injuries are present, the nature of those injuries can tell investigators a lot about what happened?

Q: Those injuries can also indicate what did not happen?

Q: Persons who make false rape allegations and support the claim with injuries tend to present a similar pattern of wounds and behavior?

Q: False victims may be indifferent to their injuries?

Q: Injuries are often self-inflicted with fingernails?

Q: Injuries are often self-inflicted with instruments commonly used by the false victim?

Q: Injuries often do not impact sensitive areas of the body like the nipples or the groin?

Q: The location of the injuries are often inconsistent with defensive wounds?

Q: When sharp or pointed weapons are used, the injuries are often cuts instead of stabs?

Q: When cuts are inflicted, there may be hesitation wounding?

Point: False victims usually have personality problems.

Q: A person who makes false rape allegations often has personality problems or disorders?

Q: They often have an impaired ability to cope?

Q: The false victim often has a pattern of difficulties in their relationships?

Q: The false victim may have a history of mental or emotional problems?

Q: The false victim may have previously reported an assault or rape with similar circumstances?

Q: The false victim's allegation may follow a recently publicized crime?

Q: The false victim's friends may report behavior that is inconsistent with the complainant's allegations?

Q: The complainant may have had recent stress-creating experiences?

Point: Other red flags regarding false victims.

Q: Persons who make false rape allegations may display an abnormal amount of dissatisfaction with how the authorities are handling the case?

Q: Persons who make false rape allegations may continuously recall additional information?

Q: Persons who make false rape allegations may display symmetrical injuries?

Q: Persons who make false rape allegations may ask for clothing to be returned to them?

Q: Persons who make false rape allegations may claim that the right questions are not being asked of them?

Point: Investigators should confront suspected false victims.

Q: When a false claim of rape is suspected, and there are questions about the truth of a report, a confrontation sometimes has to take place?

Q: How to handle the confrontation is a serious issue?

Q: A confrontation often destroys any relationship between the complainant and the confronting interviewer?

Q: One method of handling this is to introduce a second party to act as a buffer?

Q: A supervisor or coworker of the investigator can fill this role?

Q: This confrontational interview should be separate from the interviews done by the primary investigator?

Q: In a confrontational interview, it is often effective to present the doubts based on the evidence?

Q: It is often effective to present doubts in a way that is clear those doubts were based on information provided by the individual herself?

Q: The reaction of false victims when confronted can vary?

Q: At the low end, the victim may confess?

Q: Other false victims may stick to their statements in the face of overwhelming evidence?

Q: At the extreme end, the complainant may need to believe that what they are saying is true?

Q: In these circumstances, the complainant will be increasingly in denial?

Q: The complainant may react with outrage?

FALSE CONFESSIONS

Point: Investigators interview suspects to build their trust.

Q: When an investigator meets with a suspect, it is common to treat the meeting like an interview, not an interrogation?

Q: An interview format allows you to develop a rapport with the suspect?

Q: An interview format can make rapport easier to develop because the questions are non-threatening?

Q: An interview format allows the investigator to suggest the suspect is helping the investigator solve the crime?

Q: If you move from an interview to an interrogation, the questions become more aggressive?

Q: The goal of an interrogation is to get a suspect to confess to committing a crime?

Q: A police interrogation is supposed to be stressful for the suspect?

Q: It is stressful whether the suspect is guilty or innocent?

Q: A successful interrogation persuades the suspect that confessing is the only option?

Point: False confessions do happen.

Q: False confessions do happen?

Q: A false confession is when a suspect gives law enforcement incriminating information that isn't true?

Q: To lay persons, false confessions might seem irrational?

Q: But innocent people still confess to crimes/acts they did not commit?

Q: It isn't possible to accurately estimate how often false confessions occur?

Q: There are no modern studies that give accurate estimates?

Q: Regardless of how often false confessions occur, it is well settled that they do occur in our society?

Q: Even people who are mentally normal sometimes make false confessions?

Q: Even people who are psychologically normal sometimes make false confessions?

Point: Several factors lead to false confessions.

Q: Several factors lead to false confessions?

Q: The most common factors are improper use of interrogation techniques?

Q: For example, making false promises to the suspect can lead to a false confession?

Q: Promising immunity in exchange for a confession could lead to a false confession?

Q: Poor training can also lead to a false confession?

Point: Overview of interrogation structure.

Q: Interrogations are a two-step process?

Q: As the interrogator moves through the two steps, he tries to structure a suspect's perception about the nature of his situation?

Q: The interrogator also tries to structure a suspect's perception about the choices the suspect has?

Q: The goal of the first step of an interrogation is to make the suspect believe their situation is hopeless?

Q: The interrogator does this by leading the suspect to believe they've been caught?

Q: The interrogator leads the suspect to believe their guilt can be proven?

Q: The interrogator leads the suspect to believe there is no way out of their predicament?

Q: In order to do this, the investigator has to presume the suspect is guilty?

Q: There are several interrogation techniques to lead a suspect to believe they've been caught?

Q: The interrogator might accuse the suspect of having committed the crime?

Q: The interrogator might ignore any assertions of innocence by the suspect?

Q: If the suspect offers an alibi, the interrogator might suggest it is implausible?

Q: The interrogator might also suggest the alibi is contradicted by the evidence?

Q: The interrogator might suggest there is irrefutable evidence of the suspect's guilt?

Q: The interrogator might say there is physical evidence that the suspect is guilty, even when that evidence doesn't exist?

Q: The interrogator may lie to the suspect and claim physical evidence links him to the crime?

Q: Even when no physical evidence exists?

Q: The interrogator may lie to the suspect and claim eyewitnesses link him to the crime?

Q: Even when no eyewitnesses exist?

Q: The interrogator may lie to the suspect and claim forensic evidence links him to the crime?

Q: Even when no forensic evidence exists?

Q: The purpose of saying all this is to convince the suspect that his guilt can be established beyond a reasonable doubt?

Q: The goal of the second step of the interrogation is to convince the suspect that his best option is to confess?

Q: The interrogator persuades the suspect that the benefits of admitting guilt outweigh the benefits of continuing to assert innocence?

Q: The interrogator might suggest the suspect will receive some sort of benefit if he confesses to the crime?

Q: Sometimes, the interrogator will suggest that the suspect will feel better if he confesses?

Q: An interrogator might suggest this if they believe the suspect has a guilty conscience?

Q: An interrogator might also suggest this if the suspect appears anxious?

Q: The interrogator might suggest that the suspect's friends will view him as a better person if he confesses?

Q: The interrogator might suggest that the suspect's family will view him as a better person if he confesses?

Q: The interrogator might focus on how law enforcement could influence the suspect's case?

Q: The interrogator might suggest that the suspect's case will get favorable treatment if the suspect admits guilt and cooperates?

Q: The interrogator might even suggest that he's the suspect's ally?

Q: The interrogator might express a willingness to tell others about the suspect's willingness to cooperate if the suspect confesses?

Point: Interrogator training minimizes false confessions.

Q: To minimize the chance of false confession, law enforcement officers who conduct interrogations need to be properly trained?

Q: Officers need to be trained about the existence of false confessions?

Q: Officers need to be trained in the causes of false confessions?

Q: Officers need to be trained in the psychology of interrogation methods?

Q: Officers need to be trained in the effects of those interrogation methods?

Q: Officers need to be trained in the variety of false confessions that can be produced by an interrogation?

Q: Officers also need to know how to distinguish between reliable and unreliable statements?

Q: Officers should rely on objective standards for evaluating a confession?

Q: Valid confessions are usually supported by logic and evidence?

Q: The proper way to test the reliability of a confession is to analyze whether a suspect's narrative of the crime is corroborated by existing evidence?

Q: If the confession is consistent with the facts of the crime, then it may reveal the suspect has guilty knowledge of the crime?

Q: Officers need to make sure they do all in their power to corroborate the confession?

Q: True confessions often provide information that leads to corroborating evidence?

Q: False confessions do not lead to corroborating evidence?

Point: There are various types of false confessions.

Q: How an officer tests the reliability of a false confession depends on the nature of the false confession?

Q: There are different types of false confessions?

Point: Define voluntary false confession.

Q: When a suspect offers a false confession without an interrogation or in response to minor police pressure, it is called a voluntary false confession?

Q: Suspects volunteer false confessions without police questioning for a variety of reasons?

Q: Some suspects volunteer false confessions out of a desire for attention or fame?

Q: High profile crimes can attract hundreds of voluntary false confessions?

Q: Some suspects volunteer false confessions to protect the actual offender?

Q: Some suspects volunteer false confessions because they can't distinguish between fantasy and reality?

Q: Some suspects volunteer false confessions out of a desire for self-punishment?

Q: An officer can use different methods to test the trustworthiness of a confession like this?

Q: The officer can determine whether the confession leads to the discovery of evidence unknown to law enforcement?

Q: The officer can determine whether the confession identifies unusual elements of the crime that haven't been made public?

Q: The officer can determine whether the statement accurately describes small details from the crime scene that aren't easily guessed?

Q: The officer can determine whether the statement accurately describes details from the crime scene that weren't made public?

Point: Define stress-compliant false confession.

Q: One type of false confession is called a stress-compliant false confession?

Q: Stress-compliant false confessions are given when a suspect is overwhelmed by the pressure of the interrogation?

Q: Stress-compliant false confessions are given when the suspect comes to believe that the only way to end the stress is by confessing?

Q: There are three potential sources of stress during the interrogation?

Q: One source of stress is the environment of the interrogation?

Q: During an interrogation, a suspect is placed in an unfamiliar setting?

Q: The suspect is isolated from other people?

Q: The interrogator controls the pace of the interrogation?

Q: The interrogator controls the length of the questioning?

Q: The interrogator controls the intensity of the questioning?

Q: The environment of an interrogation is structured to produce stress?

Q: Another source of stress in an interrogation can be the interrogator's personal style?

Q: The interrogator can be confrontational?

Q: The interrogator can be demanding?

Q: The interrogator can be insistent?

Q: The interrogator can alternate between being confrontational, demanding, or insistent?

Q: Another source of stress is the technique and strategy used by the officers making the interrogation?

Q: Those techniques and strategies may be designed to induce anxiety in the suspect?

Q: Those techniques and strategies might attack the suspect's self-confidence?

Q: Those techniques and strategies might include appearing to ignore the suspect when he claims he's innocent?

Q: Under the stress of the interrogation, an innocent person may make a false confession if they feel the prospect of more interrogation is intolerable?

Q: If an officer suspects that a person is confessing just to end the interrogation, the officer should attempt to corroborate the confession?

Q: The officer can corroborate the confession by asking for information about the crime that only the police and the true offender know about?

Q: If the suspect can't provide that kind of information, the officer should not treat the confession as reliable?

Q: If the confession is unreliable, the officer should confront the suspect about his motivation to confess?

Point: Define coerced-compliant false confession.

Q: One type of false confession is called the coerced-compliant false confession?

Q: Coerced-compliant false confessions happen when the suspect knowingly confesses falsely?

Q: The suspect knowingly confesses falsely because of threats or promises made by the interrogators?

Q: In coerced-compliant false confessions, the suspect decides to falsely confess to end the interrogation or gain a reward?

Q: Officers should avoid making threats to the well-being of a suspect to prevent these kinds of false confessions?

211

Q: Officers can prevent these confessions by not making promises they are not legally empowered to make?

Point: Define coerced-persuaded false confession.

Q: One type of false confession is called a coerced-persuaded false confession?

Q: Coerced-persuaded false confessions occur when a detective refuses to accept the suspect's report that they don't remember committing the crime?

Q: Coerced-persuaded false confessions occur when the interrogator uses techniques which cause the suspect to doubt the reliability of their own memory?

Q: In response to these techniques, some suspects falsely believe they must have committed the crime even if they have no memory of it?

Q: The result of this false belief is a false confession from the suspect?

Q: There are techniques to identify a coerced-persuaded false confession?

Q: One technique to identify these kinds of false confessions is to look at the language of the confession?

Q: A coerced-persuaded false confession is made in hypothetical or speculative language?

Q: A suspect making a coerced-persuaded false confession may state that he may have, could have, or probably did commit the crime?

Q: This suggests the suspect lacks memory or knowledge of having committed the crime?

Q: If an officer hears language like this, they should be careful not to assist the suspect in constructing the confession?

Q: The officer should avoid answering the suspect's questions about the crime?

Q: The officer should avoid filling in blanks in the suspect's narrative about the crime?

Q: The officer should determine whether the information offered by the suspect could have been obtained from other police officers?

Q: The officer should determine whether the information offered by the suspect could have been obtained from the media?

Q: The officer should determine whether the information offered by the suspect could have been obtained from members of the community?

Point: Define non-coerced persuaded false confession.

Q: One kind of false confession is called the non-coerced persuaded false confession?

Q: Non-coerced persuaded false confessions can occur when factors other than the officer or the interrogation environment lead the suspect to believe they committed the crime?

Q: This belief is often temporary?

Q: This belief is false?

Q: The result of this false belief is a false confession from the suspect?

Q: There are techniques to identify a non-coerced persuaded false confession?

Q: One technique to identify these kinds of false confessions is to look at the language of the confession?

Q: A non-coerced persuaded false confession is made in hypothetical or speculative language?

Q: A suspect making a non-coerced persuaded false confession may state that he may have, could have, or probably did commit the crime?

Q: This suggests the suspect lacks memory or knowledge of having committed the crime?

Q: If an officer hears language like this, they should be careful not to assist the suspect in constructing the confession?

Q: The officer should avoid answering the suspect's questions about the crime?

Q: The officer should avoid filling in blanks in the suspect's narrative about the crime?

Q: The officer should determine whether the information offered by the suspect could have been obtained from other police officers?

Q: The officer should determine whether the information offered by the suspect could have been obtained from the media?

Q: The officer should determine whether the information offered by the suspect could have been obtained from members of the community?

CHAPTER 7: CROSS EXAMINING BYSTANDERS/ FRIENDS

Point: Witness was sober, able to observe and remember what happened.

Q: On the night in question you did not drink alcohol?

Q: You were the designated driver?

Q: You were sober?

Q: You were able to observe your surroundings?

Q: You did observe your surroundings?

Q: You kept an eye out for your friends?

Q: You made sure nothing bad happened to them?

Q: As you sit here today you have a clear memory of what happened that night?

Q: You have a vivid memory of what happened that night?

Point: Witness watched the victim and accused interact and saw nothing out of the ordinary.

Q: You were with them the entire night?

Q: You saw the accused there?

Q: You watched him interact with the victim?

Q: They talked?

Q: They laughed?

Q: They danced?

Q: They seem to be having a good time?

Q: They appeared happy?

Q: You didn't see him assault her?

Q: You didn't see him grab her?

Q: You didn't hear him threaten her?

Q: You didn't see him attack her?

Q: If you'd seen him attack her, you would have intervened?

Q: If you'd seen him attack her, you would have reported it?

Q: If you'd seen him sexually assault her, you would have intervened?

Q: If you'd seen him sexually assault her, you would have reported it?

Q: Based on what you observed that night, you did not report a crime?

Q: Based on what you observed that night, you did not report a sexual assault?

Point: The roommate would have heard a struggle but did not.

When a victim claims to have been sexually assaulted and that they fought, yelled, screamed, and/or resisted, it is important to find out what the roommate(s) heard. This cross is of a roommate who would have heard the struggle but did not.

Q: You were present in the apartment on the night of the alleged assault?

Q: You are the victim's roommate?

Q: She is your friend?

Q: You have known her for 2 years?

Q: You have lived with her for one year?

Q: You were in your room on the night of the alleged assault?

Q: You were watching TV?

Q: Your room is next to her bedroom?

Q: Your rooms are separated by a wall?

Q: The wall is made out of wood paneling?

Q: You can hear through the wall?

Q: When she is watching TV, you can hear it through the wall?

Q: If she is talking on the phone, you can hear it through the wall?

Q: In the past, you have asked her to turn down the TV in her room because it was too loud?

Q: You asked her to turn down her TV, by yelling through the wall?

Q: She heard you and turned it down?

Q: On the night in question, you were watching The Bachelor?

Q: You were alone in your room?

Q: She was with the accused in her room?

Q: You did not hear her TV that night?

Q: You did not hear her scream that night?

Q: You did not hear her call for help that night?

Q: You did not hear her say "no" or "stop" that night?

Q: You did not hear a struggle that night?

Q: You heard nothing out of the ordinary that night?

Q: You did hear her talking to the accused through the wall?

Q: It sounded like normal conversation?

Q: If you heard screams or cries for help, you would have reacted?

Q: You would have called the police?

Q: You would have knocked on her door?

Q: You would have tried to help?

AUTHOR BIOGRAPHIES

Michael Waddington

....

Michael is a criminal defense lawyer and former Army JAG attorney. He has defended cases in courtrooms worldwide, including in Japan, South Korea, Germany, Iraq, Bahrain, Italy, England, and the United States. He has defended some of the highest-profile court-martial cases from the "War on Terror" and has been reported on and quoted by hundreds of major media sources worldwide.

Michael is a Life Member of the National Association of Criminal Defense Lawyers (NACDL) and a Fellow of the American Board of Criminal Lawyers (ABCL). He is licensed to practice law in Florida, Georgia, Pennsylvania, New Jersey, and South Carolina. He has lectured on trial strategy and cross-examination at national CLE events, including NACDL, the National Trial Lawyers Summit, and Gideon's Promise.

He authored *Kick-Ass Closings: A Guide to Giving the Best Closing Argument of Your Life*. In 2020, he published his first legal thriller, *Battlemind*. He co-authored *Pattern Cross-Examination Questions for Expert Witnesses* and *Pattern Cross-Examination for Expert Witnesses*. He also authored the Amazon bestseller *The Art of Trial Warfare: Winning at Trial Using Sun Tzu's The Art of War*.

Michael has provided consultation services to CNN, 60 Minutes, ABC Nightline, the BBC, CBS, and the Golden Globe-winning TV series, *The Good Wife*. He appeared in a CNN documentary, *Killings at the Canal*. Some of his cases have inspired books and movies, including the Academy Award-winning documentary *Taxi to the Dark Side*, the documentary *The Kill Team*, and Brian De Palma's *Redacted*. Since 2013, Mr. Waddington has written chapters in the American Bar Association's annual publication, *The State of Criminal Justice*.

Alexandra González-Waddington

Alexandra is a criminal defense lawyer and the managing partner of the Florida-based law firm González & Waddington, LLC. She has represented hundreds of clients charged with sexual crimes and has worked on some of the most notorious war crime cases stemming from the Iraq and Afghanistan wars. A former Public Defender in the State of Georgia, Alexandra has worked on various types of cases, including rapes, violent crimes, and white-collar crimes. She is licensed to practice law in Florida and Georgia.

Alexandra graduated from Temple University's Beasley School of Law in Philadelphia, PA, where she completed Temple's Nationally ranked Integrated Trial Advocacy Program. She has also lectured on cross-examination and trial strategy at the National Trial Lawyers Summit, and NACDL's annual Sexual Assault Defense CLE conference.

Alexandra co-authored the books *Pattern Cross-Examination Questions for Expert Witnesses* and *Pattern Cross-Examination for Expert Witnesses*. Since 2015, she has written chapters in the American Bar Association's annual publication, *The State of Criminal Justice*. This annual publication examines significant issues, trends, and changes in the criminal justice system and is one of the cornerstones of the ABA's Criminal Justice Section's work. This publication serves as an invaluable resource for policy-makers, academics, and criminal justice system students.

REFERENCES

Atlas of Sexual Violence, Tara Henry - Elsevier Mosby - 2012

The California Medical Protocol for Examination of Sexual Assault and Child Sexual Abuse Victims, Office of Criminal Justice Planning - 2001

Cross-examination: Science and Techniques, Larry Pozner - Roger Dodd - LexisNexis - 2004

Evaluation and Management of the Sexually Assaulted or Sexually Abused, Patient American College of Emergency Physicians - 2013

A National Protocol for Sexual Assault Medical Forensic Examinations Adults/Adolescents, U.S. Dept. of Justice, Office on Violence Against Women - 2013

Practical Aspects of Rape Investigation: a Multidisciplinary Approach, Robert Hazelwood - Ann Burgess - CRC Press - 2008

Preventing Crime Scene Contamination, http://www.forensicmag.com/article/2014/01/preventing-crime-scene-contamination

Rape Investigation Handbook, John Savino - Brent Turvey - John Baeza - Academic Press - 2005

Notes:

Made in the USA
Columbia, SC
30 March 2025

55874076R00135